Homemade cookbook

The Best Recipes and Secrets to Master the Art of Italian Pizza Making

Owen Conti

Copyright - 2020 -

All rights reserved.

The content contained within this book may not be reproduced, duplicated or transmitted without direct written permission from the author or the publisher.

Under no circumstances will any blame or legal responsibility be held against the publisher, or author, for any damages, reparation, or monetary loss due to the information contained within this book. Either directly or indirectly.

Legal Notice:

This book is copyright protected. This book is only for personal use. You cannot amend, distribute, sell, use, quote or paraphrase any part, or the content within this book, without the consent of the author or publisher.

Disclaimer Notice:

Please note the information contained within this document is for educational and entertainment purposes only. All effort has been executed to present accurate, up to date, and reliable, complete information. No warranties of any kind are declared or implied. Readers acknowledge that the author is not engaging in the rendering of legal, financial, medical or professional advice. The content within this book has been derived from various sources. Please consult a licensed professional before attempting any techniques outlined in this book.

By reading this document, the reader agrees that under no circumstances is the author responsible for any losses, direct or indirect, which are incurred as a result of the use of information contained within this document, including, but not limited to, - errors, omissions, or inaccuracies.

Table of Contents

Introduction	6
• Chapter 1: The Preparation of the Various Types of Dough	10
Classic Pizza Dough	11
Dough with Potatoes	
Dough with Pizza Potatoes and Mediterranean Focaccia	12
Black Charcoal Mixture	13
Sweet Pizza Dough	14
Roman Dough	15
Cereal Dough	
Multi-grain pizza dough	17
Gluten-Free Pizza Dough	18
Spelt Pizza Dough	20
Kamut Pizza Dough	21
Traditional Italian All-Purpose Dough	22
Classic Thin Crust Pizza Dough	23
24-Hour Herbed Artisan Dough	24
Italian Cheese Dough	25
Whole Wheat Pizza Dough	26
Rustic Countryside Dough	28
• Chapter 2: How to Prepare the Two Most Eaten Doughs in Italy	30
Classic Dough	31

WHOLE WHEAT DOUGH	**33**
• **CHAPTER 3:**	
HOW TO PREPARE TOMATO SAUCE	**38**
BLACK CHARCOAL MIXTURE	**39**
• **CHAPTER 4:**	
CLASSIC ITALIAN PIZZAS	**42**
WHOLE WHEAT DOUGH	**43**
MARINARA PIZZA	**47**
ROMANA PIZZA	**49**
4 CHEESES PIZZA	**51**
4 SEASONS PIZZA	**52**
SICILIANA PIZZA	**54**
DIAVOLA PIZZA	**56**
ORTOLANA PIZZA	**57**
NAPOLETANA PIZZA	**59**
TUNA AND ONIONS PIZZA	**61**
CAPRICCIOSA PIZZA	**63**
SEAFOOD PIZZA	**65**
SEA AND MOUNTAINS PIZZA	**67**
HAM AND MUSHROOMS PIZZA	**69**
APULIAN PIZZA	**70**
TYROLEAN PIZZA	**71**
BOSCAIOLA PIZZA	**74**
CALZONE	**76**
• **CHAPTER 5:**	
SPECIAL PIZZAS	**80**
FRIED PIZZA	**81**
GLUTEN-FREE PIZZA	**83**
PIZZA AND MORTAZZA	**85**
FRIED PIZZELLE	**87**
RED PIZZAS	**90**

Pizza Roll 92
Fried Pizza with Mortadella and Fiordilatte 95
Pear and Brie Pizza 98
Pizza with Mortadella and Buffalo Mozzarella 100
Mascarpone Pizza, Speck and Walnuts 102
Wallet Pizza with Salami 105
Fried Panzerotti 108
- Chapter 6: Types of Cooking 112

Conclusion 120

Introduction

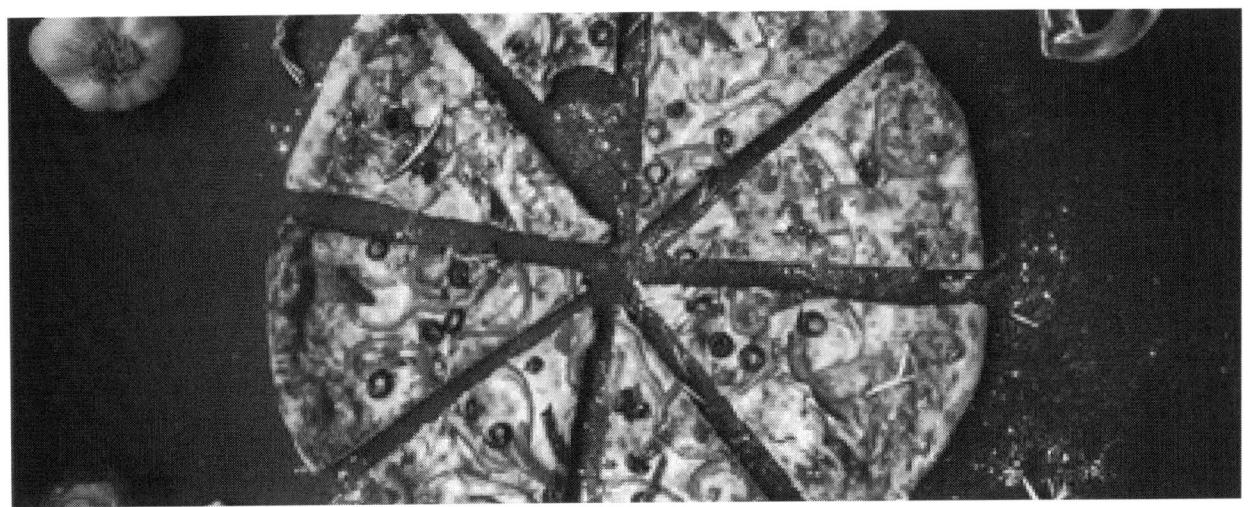

What exactly could someone not like about the pizza? Savory dough topped with a bucket-load of cheese and tomato sauce. For any picky eater in your home, pizza is the best and ultimate dish.

For children, pizza is often counted as one of their favorite foods, while for adults it is counted as one of the most convenient meals around. From the ability to add the toppings you like, there is rarely a type of pizza that isn't loved by at least one person.

Italy is known for its gift of pizza to the culinary world. Italian pizzas are considered authentic with a range of healthy topping options. Italians have also their unique technique of preparing pizzas.

I sincerely believe that pizza is a healthy food, except for the gluten, right? Call me crazy, but I never feel bad after eating pizza. I usually can stay fit and trim when eating pizza two times per week. Think about what the main ingredients consist of. You've got the flour, water, yeast, and tomatoes with a touch of olive oil here and there.

And no, if you're thinking that the fast-food chain restaurant pizza is just as healthy, it's most likely not. They probably add artificial ingredients and dough conditioners to make the dough very soft after it's baked.

My belief is that a pizza is healthy because it isn't fried in oil like French Fries that sit in extremely hot oil, which can cause a myriad of health problems. It's baked in an oven. Baked items are usually always healthier than deep-fried. Fresh pizza made daily usually doesn't have dough conditioners if they make the dough by hand, since it's not a pre-made pizza crust that you buy in the store.

The only thing that I can think of as healthier is if you could find a gluten-free pizza shop. There's not that many of them, but they're out there. So, try a slice one day at one of these places if they sell it by the slice. If not try a small pie to see if you like it.

Gluten is known to can cause health issues in many people, so you may want to lay off the real stuff and try some gluten-free pizza one of these days. I tasted it fresh once and it was delicious.

If you love pizza and have always wanted to make pizza within the comfort of your own home, then you have certainly come to the right place. Inside of this in-depth pizza cookbook, you will learn every aspect of pizza making, from making the dough correctly, to rising the dough, preparing the sauce to even pairing the pizza with the perfect toppings.

Italian pizzas are the most famous and traditional pizzas around the world. Various chefs belonging to other countries try to imitate the recipe of an Italian pizza so they can amaze the world with their expertise in pizza making. The part of this book containing the top pizza recipes of Italian history will guide you on how to create Italian masterpieces in your kitchen.

By the end of this book and with the help of the pizza recipes, you will become a pizza making pro in no time.

Chapter 1: The Preparation of the Various Types of Dough

Classic Pizza Dough

Ingredients

- 250 g Water
- 500 g 0 flour
- 2 tbsp. Salt
- 2-3 g Brewer's yeast, fresh
- 2 tbsps. Extra virgin olive oil

Directions

1. Into a bowl, pour in oil, yeast crumbs and water. Add flour and then use your hands to mix all the ingredients and after they have mixed well, add salt. The dough should be ready in 5 minutes

2. Divide the dough into 4 balls and then leave it to rest for 1 hour while it's covered with a cloth. Meanwhile, be preparing the filling ingredients.

3. Use little oil to grease at least 4 round oven containers after the leavening time is over. You can as well use the aluminum containers of 28-30 diameter. Put the balls on the top and use fingertips to press from the center going outwards. You can as well use a rolling pin when doing this operation at home.

4. Put your preferred seasonings and bake for 15 minutes in an oven preheated at 200 degrees and until the edge becomes golden. Avoid opening the door of the oven to check the degree at which the pizzas are cooking before at least 10 minutes are over because this causes heat dispersion and this will lead to having a chewy and elastic pizza.

Dough with Potatoes
Dough with Pizza Potatoes and Mediterranean Focaccia

Ingredients

- 300 g Potatoes
- 5 g Brewer's yeast
- 10 g Salt
- 10 g Sugar
- 600 g 0 flour of the Manitoba type
- 400 ml Water

Directions

1. Here you begin by preparing the potatoes. Nicely wash them and put them in a pot, put some cold water to cover them and bring them to boil for 20 minutes. The time of cooking varies based on the potato size. Skewer the potatoes using a fork to be sure of the right cooking degree.
2. Once the potatoes are ready, drain them and allow them to cool. Peel them and pass them through a potato masher until reduced to a homogeneous and creamy puree.
3. Pour the water at room temperature in a bowl and in it, dissolve the yeast. Add the potato puree, sugar, and flour gradually. Add salt too and mix everything well until an elastic and soft dough is formed.
4. Put the dough in a tightly closed container covered with a lid after dividing it into 3 balls and let it rise until it doubles in the volume, this may take few hours.
5. Roll out the dough and also season it to your preference after finishing the phase of leavening.

Black Charcoal Mixture

Ingredients

- 1 cup whole meal flour
- 2 teaspoons dried yeast
- Dash of white sugar
- 1/2 cup warm water
- 1/2 cup white flour
- 1 teaspoon salt
- 1 tablespoon olive oil
- 2 g bamboo or coconut shell activated charcoal powder (4 capsules)

Cooking: 2 h 15'
Preparation: 15'
Serves: 2

Directions

1. Stir together the sugar, yeast and warm water in a small bowl until the mixture becomes lightly bubbly or you can let it sit for 10 minutes.
2. Combine the activated charcoal powder, salt and the flour in a large bowl and stir them in the yeast.
3. On a floured surface, use your hands to knead the dough until it becomes elastic and smooth. You can now shape it into a dough ball.
4. In a large bowl, put the dough ball, use a damp towel to cover the bowl and let it sit in a warm place. Punch down on the dough's surface after one hour and again use a damp towel to cover the bowl. Leave the dough to rise again for other 45 minutes.

Sweet Pizza Dough

Preparation: 30-40'

Ingredients

- 1 cup all-purpose flour
- 1 cup 00 flour
- 1 teaspoon sugar
- ¼ teaspoon kosher salt
- ¾ cup very cold unsalted butter, cut into 12 equal cubes, divided
- ½ cup ice water

Directions

1. In a bowl fitted with the paddle attachment of a stand mixer, mix sugar, flour, and salt.
2. Add 8 of the butter cubes and mix on low speed until the butter begins to break down and the mixture has a sandy appearance. Stop the mixer and sort through the unformed dough by hand, using your fingers to pinch together any large chunks of butter that remain. Mix on low for 2 or 4 more turns. Add the remaining 4 butter cubes and again mix on low until the butter is slightly incorporated about 2 minutes. Stop the mixer and remove the work bowl. Repeat the pinching step and make sure there are no remaining large chunks of butter in the mixture.
3. Make a well in the center of the shaggy mass. Add the ice water to the well and gently cover the water pool with the surrounding dough crumbs. Let the dough stand for 5 minutes to allow it to absorb some of the water.
4. Mix the dough by hand, quickly and evenly. Knead the dough only long enough so it forms a moist, slightly sticky ball, being careful not to overwork it.
5. Divide the dough into two equal portions and wrap each in plastic wrap. Flatten each ball into a smooth disc about ½ inch thick. The dough should have a nice, even marbled appearance, streaked with butter.
6. Refrigerate the dough until ready to use, at least 2 hours and up to 24 hours.

Roman Dough

Ingredients

- 3.5 g Dried powdered yeast
- 650 ml Water at room temperature
- 20 g Sea salt
- 1 kg Whole-wheat flour, unbleached and stoneground
- 25 ml Extra virgin olive oil
- ½ tsp. sugar, superfine

Cooking: 15'
Preparation: 14'
Serves: 3
Difficult: Easy

Directions

1. In a mixer, put the flour with a dough hook attachment.
2. In 100 ml of water, dissolve the yeast and add the flour with the 400 ml water that remained and the superfine sugar.
3. Turn on the mixer to the lowest setting and mix for 2 minutes until the water is absorbed totally. Add salt and water and mix. Adding the water slowly little by little, double the mixer speed and add more water once the previous amount you put is absorbed. Don't worry if the mixture looks quite wet, just keep mixing for 8-10 minutes and the dough will gradually start stretching and it will form long gluten strands.
4. In a mixer bowl, rest the dough for 10 minutes while it's covered with a plastic wrap before you fold it. Leave it in the refrigerator to mature and form into three sheets of roman style pizza dough.

Shaping your Roman-style dough

5. When the dough has rested briefly, to give it strength, it needs to be folded.

Use a teaspoon of extra virgin olive oil to oil your hands and also oil the work surface lightly. Remove the dough from the container to a work surface. To form pockets of air, gently lift in the center and fold the ends under and meet in the middle.

6. Repeat the fold and turn the dough at 90 degrees. Cover the bowl with a plastic wrap and let it rest for 15 minutes and again fold. Leave to rest for other 15 minutes and do a final folding as before. Get a plastic container with an airtight lid and oil it and put the dough in there. Put in the refrigerator and leave for 18-24 hours.

7. When the dough matures once in the refrigerator, remove from the container and put on a work surface and divide the dough into 3 pieces.

8. To form a ball, shape each piece of dough by putting your hands under the outer edges and slide. Repeat this several times until the dough gets a ball-like appearance.

9. Using your fingers, gather and fold at the edge of every piece of dough and bring the balls towards you. This makes the ball smooth and even. Dough balls should be left to rise again for 2 hours at room temperature in three oiled contained containers.

10. Oil with extra virgin olive oil a baking tray or oven tray, on a work surface, put flour and turn one piece of dough. On the dough surface, start pressing gently using your fingers to roughly fit the tray size by stretching it.

11. Without a fan, preheat the oven to 250 degrees to cook the dough for any Roman-style pizza recipes, which require the dough.

Cereal Dough
Multi-grain pizza dough

Ingredients

- 1 cup boiling water
- 1 cup white whole wheat flour
- 1 teaspoon organic canola oil or avocado oil
- ½ cup 8-grain cereal
- 2 teaspoons pure maple syrup or honey, dark or amber
- 2 ¼ teaspoons active dry yeast
- ¾ cup bread flour or all-purpose flour
- ½ teaspoon salt

Directions

1. In a heat proof mixing bowl or a bowl of an electric stand mixer, put maple syrup/honey and cereal. Over the cereal, pour boiling water and allow it sit until warm like 105 degrees for 15 minutes.

2. Over the grains, sprinkle the yeast and allow the yeast to sit for 5 minutes until it's foamy. Add salt, whole-wheat flour and all-purpose flour. Use a dough hook to mix until they are elastic and smooth for 5 minutes.

3. Get to a lightly floured work surface and continue kneading for 8 to 10 minutes until elastic and smooth.

4. In a clean bowl, brush some oil and add dough, turn to coat with the oil. Use a plastic wrap to cover and allow it to rise and double in size. This can take 40 minutes to 1 hour. Use a bowl scraper to scrape.

Gluten-Free Pizza Dough

Cooking: 10-20'
Preparation: 2 h
Serves: 2

Ingredients

- 1 cup lukewarm water
- ¼ cup whole milk, at room temperature
- 1 tablespoon plus 2 teaspoons active dry yeast
- 1 extra-large egg
- 5¼ cups gluten-free flour
- 2 teaspoons baking powder, sifted
- 2 teaspoons kosher salt
- 2 teaspoons sugar
- 2 tablespoons extra-virgin olive oil, divided

Directions

1. In a small bowl, combine the warm water and milk. Sprinkle the yeast evenly over the surface and stir to combine. Set aside in a warm spot until active and bubbly, about 15 minutes.
2. When the yeast mixture is active and bubbly, lightly whisk in the egg.
3. Attach the paddle to your stand mixer. In the work bowl, combine the flour, baking powder, salt, and sugar and mix on low speed.
4. Add the bubbly sponge to the work bowl and mix on low speed until combined, 2 to 3 minutes.
5. Gather the dough and transfer to a not floured work surface. Briefly knead the dough to combine, 4 or 5 turns total.
6. Divide the dough into two equal portions and wrap each tightly in plastic wrap. Gently shape each into a 2-inch-thick disc. Leave to rise in a warm spot for 45 minutes.
7. Preheat the wood oven to approximately 500°F. Brush a quarter sheet pan with 1 tablespoon of the olive oil.

8. Using a wooden rolling pin, roll out the dough on a clean, dry, not floured surface to ¼-inch thickness, and transfer to the prepared sheet pan. With a sharp paring knife, trim away any excess dough that hangs over the sides of the tray. Fill in any gaps by using the trimmed pieces, pressing the seams together. The entire tray should be filled to the edges. With the tines of a fork, prick the entire surface of the dough.

9. Brush the remaining 1-tablespoon of olive oil over the top of the dough. Transfer to a warm spot and allow the dough to proof for 15 minutes before baking.

10. Bake the dough in a relatively cool zone of the oven, away from the fire, until lightly browned, 8 to 10 minutes, making sure to rotate frequently. Remove the tray from the oven and leave to cool slightly. Add the toppings of your choice and return to the hot oven and bake until warmed through, about 5 minutes more.

Spelt Pizza Dough

Cooking: 40'
Preparation: 15'
Serves: 4

Ingredients

- 2 tsps. Honey
- 1 tbsp. Extra virgin olive oil
- 1 tsp. Kosher salt
- 1 package Active dry yeast
- 3 cups sprouted spelt flour
- 1 cup of warm water

Directions

1. In a bowl, whisk water, yeast, honey and 1 cup of flour together. Let it stand for about 20 minutes until the mixture is bubbly and the yeast softens.
2. Into a yeast mixture, stir the remaining olive oil, salt, and flour.
3. In a bowl, beat the mixture that has remained using an electric mixer that has been fitted with a dough hook attachment and if necessary, add more flour until a tacky and soft dough is formed. This takes 3-4 minutes.
4. Put the dough in a mixing bowl with some olive oil and use a plate to cover the bowl and let the dough rise and dough in size, this takes like 1 hour 30 minutes.
5. Transfer the dough to a lightly floured work surface after punching it. Divide the dough into 4 balls and leave each to rest after it's covered until the dough slightly rises for like 30 to 45 minutes.
6. Finally, roll them in the desired thickness and shapes.

Kamut Pizza Dough

Ingredients

- 3 tbsps. Extra virgin olive oil
- 1 1/3 cups warm water
- 1 1/2 package dry yeast
- 1/2 tsp. Sea salt
- 4 cups Kamut flour

Cooking: 0'
Preparation: 2 h
Serves: 16

Directions

1. In a measuring cup, put together the water and oil, stir them and let them sit for 5 minutes. In a mixing bowl, put the sea salt and flour and thoroughly mix them.

2. Over the flour, pour the yeast mixture and form into the dough ball. Use your hands and knead for 10 minutes. You can as well put the dough in a food processor and to knead, pulse for 5 minutes.

3. Oil a large mixing bowl lightly using olive oil and put the dough in it. Put in a warm area after covering with a damp towel. Allow it to sit for 1-2 hours until the size doubles.

4. The dough is now ready to punch down and divide into two balls. Put the rolled-out pizza dough on a large cookie sheet or pizza pan. Use your favorite toppings to the top and let it sit for 5 minutes before you start baking.

Traditional Italian All-Purpose Dough

Ingredients

- 2 ½ teaspoons dry active yeast
- 1 cup lukewarm water
- 2 teaspoons salt
- 1 teaspoon sugar
- 4 tablespoons extra virgin olive oil
- 4 cups flour

Directions

1. In a large bowl, combine the water and the yeast. Once the yeast has dissolved add the sugar and oil and stir well.

2. Stir the salt into the flour and then place it in a mound on a clean work surface. Use your hands to make a well in the center of the flour. Slowly add the yeast mixture to the well and begin to incorporate the flour around the edges until all of the ingredients are well combined. Working quickly, knead the dough until it looks elastic and smooth.

3. Lightly oil a clean bowl and set the dough ball in it. Cover the bowl with plastic wrap and a clean kitchen towel. Set the dough in a warm spot and allow it to rise for about 2 hours. Punch the dough down and divide into at least 2 dough balls or more if you are making smaller pizzas. Cover the dough again and allow it to rise for an additional hour.

Classic Thin Crust Pizza Dough

Ingredients

- 2 tablespoons dry active yeast
- 1 cup lukewarm water
- 4 cups flour
- 2 tablespoons extra virgin olive oil
- 1 ½ teaspoons salt

Directions

1. In a large bowl, dissolve the yeast in the water. Combine the flour, oil, and salt. Then stir the flour into the yeast mixture in small batches. The dough should start to become smooth and pull away from the sides of the bowl. If it doesn't, adjust water and flour amounts as necessary.

2. Cover your work surface with a dusting of flour and quickly knead the dough until it becomes elastic and easy to work with.

3. Oil a clean bowl and place the dough in it; cover with lightly oiled plastic wrap. Allow the dough to rise in a warm spot for 1 to 3 hours or until it has doubled in size.

24-Hour Herbed Artisan Dough

Ingredients

- ½ teaspoon active dry yeast
- ¼ cup lukewarm water
- 3 cups flour
- 1 cup milk
- 2 ½ tablespoons olive oil
- 1 teaspoon salt
- 2 tablespoons chopped basil
- 2 tablespoons chopped oregano

Directions

1. Place the yeast in lukewarm water until foamy. Then combine the yeast mixture and flour in a large mixing bowl by whisking together. Then add the milk and the oil. Use your hands to mix the ingredients until a loose dough forms; add the salt and herbs. Knead a couple of times no more until ball forms. If the dough is sticky it's okay.

2. Into an oiled bowl, let the dough ball and cover with oiled wax paper followed by a layer of plastic wrap. Let the bowl in a warm place for 24 hours. 3 to 4 hours before the 24 hour period is complete, carefully turn the dough ball in the bowl and recover to finish rising.

Italian Cheese Dough

Ingredients

- 1 cup lukewarm water
- ¼ cup olive oil, plus additional
- 1 teaspoon honey
- 2 ¼ teaspoons active dry yeast
- 3 cups flour, plus additional
- 1/2 cup freshly grated Parmigiano-Reggiano cheese

Directions

1. In a large bowl, combine the water, oil, and honey; sprinkle yeast on top. The mixture should have a foamy appearance after 5 to 8 minutes.

2. In a separate bowl, mix together the flour and cheese. Slowly add the flour mixture to the yeast mixture, stirring as you go. The dough should be soft and a bit sticky so adjust water and flour amounts as necessary. Keep mixing until the dough begins to have an elastic appearance.

3. Flour your work surface and begin to knead the dough just until it becomes smooth. Oil a large bowl and place your dough in it, turning it several times to make sure the dough gets oiled lightly on all sides. Place oiled plastic wrap over the bowl and set it in a warm location. Allow the dough to rise until it has more than doubled in size (about 1 to 3 hours).

4. Before using the dough, knead on a floured work area for another minute so that it returns to a smooth and elastic state and so that any extra oil gets absorbed.

Whole Wheat Pizza Dough

Ingredients

- 1 cup lukewarm water
- ¼ cup olive oil
- 1 teaspoon sugar
- 2 ¼ teaspoons active dry yeast
- 2 ¼ cups flour
- ¾ cup whole wheat flour
- ¼ teaspoon salt

Directions

1. In a large bowl, combine the water, oil, and sugar; sprinkle yeast on top. The mixture should have a foamy appearance when it's ready, about 5 to 8 minutes.

2. In a separate bowl, sift the flours together with the salt. Working slowly, begin to add the flour mixture to the yeast mixture, adding just a little at a time and stirring constantly. Adjust flour or water amounts appropriately so that your dough looks soft and just a bit sticky.

3. Flour your work surface and quickly knead the dough until it becomes smooth – don't overwork it. Oil a clean bowl and put the dough in it, turning a few times so that all sides of the dough are covered lightly with oil. Cover the bowl with oiled plastic wrap and place in a warm spot. Let the dough rise until it has doubled in size (1 to 3 hours depending on how warm the spot is).

4. Before using the dough, knead on a floured work area for another minute so that it returns to a smooth and elastic state and so that any extra oil gets absorbed

Advice

Pizza dough made with whole-wheat flour takes twice as much time to rise.

The whole meal flours absorb much water than refined flours. For that matter, the water amounts on the recipe are just indicative and it's upon you to feel the dough consistency obtained and add little water if it is too hard.

To get an easier product to work on, most of the dough is made by adding a percentage of refined flour and a percentage of whole-wheat flour.

Rustic Countryside Dough

Ingredients

- 4 cups flour
- 1 small potato, boiled, peeled, and mashed
- 6 tablespoons lukewarm water
- ½ cup pale lager
- 2 tablespoons dry active yeast
- 3 tablespoons extra virgin olive oil
- Salt, to taste

Directions

1. Allow the yeast to dissolve in the water.
2. In a large mixing bowl, combine the flour, mashed potato, yeast mixture and beer; mix thoroughly. As a loose dough starts to form, add the oil and salt. Once the dough begins to pull away from the sides of the bowl, place on a floured work surface and knead until elastic.
3. Place the dough in an oiled bowl and cover it using a plastic wrap. In a warm spot, let the dough rise for about 2 hours or until it doubles in the size.
4. Note that this dough tends to bake a little longer than others so be sure not to take it out too soon!

Chapter 2: How to Prepare the Two Most Eaten Doughs in Italy

Classic Dough

Ingredients

- 300 g 00 flour
- 35 g Extra virgin olive oil
- 200 g Manitoba flour
- 10 g Salt
- 5 g Fresh brewer's yeast
- 300 ml Water at room temperature

Difficult: Easy

Preparation: 20'

Serves: 2

Cost: Very low

Note: Rising time 2 hours.

Directions

1. In preparing the pizza dough, you can use the hand to mix everything but if you choose to use a mixer, you follow the same procedures at medium-low speed using the hook. Get the water at room temperature and pour the yeast into it. You can as well crumble the yeast in the flour, the result remains the same. You can choose to use 2 g of beer yeast that is dehydrated upon preference.

2. Pour the 00 flour and the Manitoba in a container and while you are kneading; keep adding some water little at a time. The recommended water temperature should be 25 degrees. After pouring half the liquid, add salt and keep mixing while pouring in water little by little until you get a homogeneous mixture.

3. While continuing to knead, you can add some oil and keep adding little at a time. Lastly is transferring the dough to a work surface and you continue using your hands to work on it until it is homogeneous and smooth.

4. When you get a nice and smooth dough, allow it to rest for about 10 minutes on the work surface. Use a bowl to cover it. Give it a small fold once it has rested. Divide it into 4 parts and gently pull each one and fold it towards the center and give it a sphere shape.

5. The dough that has been formed, transfer it to a bowl, use a plastic wrap to cover it and allow it to rise. You can put the bowl in the oven with lights off for convenience. The temperature ideal for leavening is at least 26-28 degrees. You can alternatively keep the bowl in a warm place. Weather and temperature influence the leavening of the dough but averagely the dough should take 2 hours to double.

6. The dough will be nicely swollen after the rising time elapses. Just transfer it to the worktop and use tarot to divide it into halves. You can flour the work surface lightly if needed.

Storage:

The dough can be preserved or cooked once it has risen. In a case like this, you can reduce the yeast amount significantly, use a cling film to cover the bowl and put it in a refrigerator for 8-12 hours for it to mature. Just leave the dough to acclimatize once the time elapses and continue per the recipe.

Pizza dough can also be frozen once it has been leavened. You can store it in a frosting bag after dividing it into desired portions then it will be enough to allow the portion thaw at room temperature then you continue per the recipe.

Whole Wheat Dough

Ingredients

- 4 g Dry brewer's yeast
- 310 g Room temperature water
- 10 g Salt
- 250 g Whole meal flour
- 250 g Flour
- 10 g Acacia honey
- 30 g Extra virgin olive oil

To season:

- 10 g Extra virgin olive oil
- 125 g Mozzarella
- 200 g Tomato sauce
- Dried oregano to taste
- Salt to taste

Cook time: 25'
Preparation: 30'
Serves: 2
Cost: Very low
Note: Rising time 3 hours.

Directions

1. In a bowl, sift the whole meal flour and then add honey and dehydrated beer yeast. Using your hands, begin kneading and use water at room temperature to pour there. Keep kneading until you get a homogeneous mixture. The dough will become very liquid.

2. Use a plastic wrap to cover and allow it to rise in an oven with lights turned on for at least an hour. Take the dough again once it has leavened, sieve it in another bowl, add some flour and add to the leavened dough.

3. Keep kneading with your hands and when the mixture becomes compact, add some olive oil and salt and keep kneading. As soon as the oil has

absorbed and the dough is compact, transfer it to a lightly oiled work surface and use your hands to work on it until it becomes smooth. Give folds to the dough. This serves in giving them more leavening momentum.

4. Use the dough to form a ball and put it in a lightly oiled bowl, use a cling film to cover and allow it to rise. Put it in the oven with lights on until it doubles in volume or for at least 2 hours. When the time for leavening ends, use tarot to divide the dough into two equal parts of 400 g.

5. Get 32 cm diameter pizza trays and grease them. Put the two dough balls and allow them to rest for 10 minutes while they are not spread.

Storage:

It is recommended to eat the whole meal pizza still fresh. It can also be brought halfway when cooking, allow it cool then freeze it. It must be allowed to thaw at room temperature before use and complete cooking it in the oven before serving.

Advice:

When you make small pizzas with this dough, they become a genuine and tasty snack for the old and young.

Essential Tips for Perfect Homemade Pizza Dough

- Dissolve yeast in lukewarm water

Be careful not to let the water get too hot when adding yeast too hot of water above 115 degrees F will kill it. Dissolving yeast in water before you use it to make the dough is also a great way to double-check that the yeast is still good. If your yeast doesn't expand then it's too old and your crust won't turn out very well.

- Salt and yeast don't get along

Don't add salt directly to a liquid yeast mixture wait until the yeast gets worked into the flour.

- Don't use too much whole grain flour

The best pizza dough is made with a combination of white bread flour and a bit of whole wheat 3/4 cup white and ¼ cup whole wheat is the best ratio. If you use too much whole grain flour you will end up with heavy crust.

- Adjust ingredient amounts slowly

If you feel like the dough is too sticky, add a bit of flour. If it seems too stiff, more water is the answer. The key is to be very careful when you start adjusting ratios. Work slowly and in tiny amounts, 1 teaspoon of water or flour goes a long way.

- Perfect pizza dough is elastic

Don't be satisfied with your dough unless it has a great elastic feel and appearance. If it looks lumpy or is falling apart it's not going to taste good once it's cooked, keep trying.

- Don't over knead your dough

This is one of the biggest pitfalls when it comes to making the perfect pizza dough at home. You should not knead your dough for more than a minute or two. If we're getting technical 70 seconds seems to have the best results. I know kneading is fun, but too much playing results in a super tough crust.

- Always allow your dough to rise in a warm place in an oiled bowl

Most recipes will tell you this, but in case they don't or unless they have a compelling case you should always lightly oil your bowl and the top of the dough before allowing it to rise. Be aware of the surface you're putting your dough on as well the top of a pre-heating oven, while warm, can get too hot and your dough can actually start cooking rather than rising.

- Cover your rising dough with thick plastic wrap

The plastic wrap should allow a bit of air to pass under it, but overall should be nice and tight. This works better than any other form of coverage because it helps to keep your dough ball's environment nice and humid, which is perfect for rising.

- Rising times vary

If a recipe says: let the dough rise for an hour or until it has doubled, go with the "until it has doubled" rule. Depending on how warm the room is, dough can either rise very fast or may need more time, like 4 hours so be patient. If the dough doesn't rise appropriately you can guarantee that your crust will suffer.

- Be cautious with your dough once it has risen

You never want to jostle dough in this state around. So walk slowly, don't drop it, don't whack it, and never use a knife to cut it if it needs to be divided.

Chapter 3: How to Prepare Tomato Sauce

Black Charcoal Mixture

Ingredients

- Salt
- 500 g San Marzano tomatoes
- Sodium bicarbonate
- Garlic cloves
- Basil
- Oregano
- Pepper

Difficult: Easy
Preparation: 15'
Serves: 6

Directions

1. To make the tomato sauce for pizza, start by washing the tomatoes and use a knife to clean them of the stalk. Add them to boiling water in a pot to blanch them. This should be for a few minutes. Remove from the water, divide into halves, peel and remove the seeds.

2. Blend the tomatoes until the pulp it is smooth and homogenous. Get the pulp and set with the other sauce.

3. Add baking soda stir to adjust the acidity. Taste to tell if the acidity is right. If sour, and more baking soda.

4. Add salt and the sauce is good to go. The recommended dose is for a pizza of 21-22 cm, use 80-90 g of sauce. This sauce is enough for 5 pizzas.

There are various variations of this recipe just like in many Italian recipes, but they do not affect the good taste. Check the following three examples:

1. Tomato sauce for mushroom pizza

Pizza with mushroom sauce is a typical pairing. The mushroom sauce gets flavor and taste to give more quality to the final dish. To make it, use 100 g of porcini or champignon mushrooms. Wash them and use a knife to cut before adding them over the sauce.

2. Tomato sauce for pizza with buffalo mozzarella

One of the classic pizza sauce combos is the mozzarella. Margherita is born on the other side. Buffalo mozzarella is used by those respecting Neapolitan tradition because it is more succulent. Slices it into tine pieces and put on the sauce. You will love it.

3. Tomato sauce for deviled pizza

The sauce is made tastier by a little spiciness. Spicy salami and hot pepper when added to your deviled pizza will make it spicy and tastier.

Chapter 4: Classic Italian Pizzas

Whole Wheat Dough

Ingredients

- 300 g 00 flour
- 200 g Manitoba flour
- 10 g Salt
- 5 g Fresh brewer's yeast
- 35 g Extra virgin olive oil
- 300 ml water

To season:
- 400 g Fiordilatte
- 1 tbsp. Dry oregano
- 500 g Tomato pulp
- Basil to taste
- 1 tsp Salt
- Extra virgin olive oil

Cook time: 15'
Preparation: 30'
Serves: 2
Cost: Low
Note: Rising time 2 h 50'
Difficulty: Medium

Directions

1. Begin by making the basic dough. Get a jug and pour in water at room temperature. Add yeast and use a teaspoon to mix until it completely dissolves.

2. You can use a planetary mixer to make the basic dough, operating it at medium-low speed and using a hook or you can use your hands to knead.

3. Combine the two flours in a bowl. Add water and begin kneading with your hands, add salt and the rest of the water that is needed. Continue using your hands to work on the mixture until a uniform result is got. At this particular point, add oil. Keep adding little by little as you continue kneading in order

to ease its absorption. Take the dough to a work surface and keep working on it vigorously for few more minutes until it's elastic and smooth.

4. Once you have got a nice and smooth dough, you can allow it to rest on a work surface for 10 minutes while it's covered with a bowl. Give it a small fold once rested. Assume that that sphere is divided in 4 parts. Pull each part gently and fold it towards the center and give it a sphere shape.

5. Put the dough that has been formed into the bowl and use a plastic wrap to cover it and allow it to rise. You can put the bowl in an oven when the lights are off to allow the inside reach a temperature of 26 to 28 degrees, that's for convenience purposes. This temperature range is good for leavening. You can as well keep the bowl in a warm place alternatively.

6. Weather conditions and temperature influence the leavening for each particular dough, but averagely, the dough should at least take 2 hours to double in its volume.

7. Transfer the dough to a work surface once it has risen well by inverting the bowl gently and using a tarot to divide it in a half. You can sprinkle the top using some little flour if it's necessary.

8. Return to giving the dough a fold like you did before rising and continue with pirling after you have turned it over. Pirling the dough refers to using your hands to make the dough turn, taking it away and moving it by bringing it towards you until you get a regular and smooth sphere.

9. Transfer the two doughs to a tray. Cover them with a cloth or a cling film and allow them to rest for 30 minutes.

10. Meanwhile, heat the oven in a static mode to 250 degrees and go prepare the filling ingredients. In a bowl, put the colander and use your hands to fray the mozzarella gradually positioning it in the colander, this will help to loosen all the serum that is excess.

11. In another bowl, pour the tomato pulp and season them with oregano, a turn of oil and salt. Mix them very well for 30 minutes and once they are over, continue with the dough.

12. Put one of the two sticks on the dusted work surface and use your hands

to slightly squeeze it and then to make a rotating movement and exert slight pressure, stretch it. Try not to crush the bubbles a lot and incase the dough becomes too elastic, before working on it again, wait for some few minutes. Lift the dough disc and put it in your hands and for it to stretch further, close it in your fist and turn it.

13. To give the dough a regular shape, use your hands to put it on a lightly greased pan of 28 cm diameter. Cook in a preheated static oven at 250 degrees on a central shelf after sprinkling half of a tomato on it for 7 minutes.

14. When this is over, remove the pizza from the oven, add fiordilatte and bake at the same temperature for 6-7 minutes.

15. Remove your pizza margherita from the oven and garnish with fresh basil leaves.

For Cooking on the Refractory Stone

If you want to use the refractory stone to cook the pizza margherita, operate the oven in grill ode at 250 degrees. Put the refractory stone on the top shelf and allow it to warm for about 30 minutes. Transfer your rolled-out pizza on a lightly floured wooden shovel, use mozzarella and tomato to season and add some oil and allow it to side on the stone and cook it for 4 minutes. This will make it even crunchier.

Storage

Pizza dough can be frozen or even stored in a frost bag after being divided in portions once it is leavened. It will then be enough to allow the portion to thaw at room temperature.

If preferred, you can cook the pizza margherita halfway and freeze it. Once cooked, let it cool, cover it with aluminum and freeze it and once still frozen, just cook it at a lower temperature.

Advice

There is no need of dividing the dough in two loaves if you want to use a rectangular pan to bake the pizza. Directly spread it inside the pan after the first leavening and before cooking or seasoning it, wait for about 20 minutes.

It could necessitate extending the times of cooking until your pizza is golden brown.

Marinara Pizza

Ingredients

- 7 g dry brewer's yeast
- 600 g water
- 1 kg 00 flour
- 60 g Extra virgin olive oil
- 20 g Salt

For the dressing:
- 4 garlic cloves
- 700 g Tomato sauce
- 20 g Dry oregano
- Black pepper to taste
- Salt to taste

Cook time: 30'
Preparation: 30'
Serves: 4
Cost: Very Low
Difficulty: Easy

Directions

1. To make the marinara pizza, begin by pouring the flour into a mixer bowl. Add 100 ml of water and yeast and then use a hook mounted at medium-low speed to operate the planetary mixer.

2. Continue by adding water little at a time and make sure you wait till the previous dose is well absorbed by the flour. When you have added at least ¾ of water, keep kneading after adding salt. Always keep adding the rest of the water flush and allow it to work until you get a homogeneous and smooth mixture.

3. Gradually add the oil at this point and remove the dough from the planetary mixer once the oil has absorbed completely and use your hands to shape it until you form a ball. Put it in a bowl that is lightly greased.

4. Use a clean cloth or a cling film to cover and allow it to rise in the oven while

lights are on. Hold on until the dough has doubled in its size but better if tripled and continue with the pizza preparation.

5. Transfer the dough to the pastry board once it rises and divide it in 4 equal parts. Do this for each of the balls. Let it stand for 30 minutes after covering it with a clean tea towel.

6. Use a drizzle of oil to lightly grease four 30 cm diameter pizza pans and put the dough ball in the center of the pan. Begin squeezing from the center outwards if necessary, pulling the sides slightly. If the dough tends to return to its original shape or it's too elastic, put aside the pizza that you spread and begin rolling another one, leave the previous one to rest. Try spreading the dough over the whole surface of the tray.

7. In a large bowl, pour in the tomato sauce and season with oil, pepper, salt and oregano. On the pizza base, pour a generous ladle of tomato sauce and spread it in a circular motion leaving only a boarder of 1.5 cm but covering almost the entire area.

8. Cut the garlic into half after peeling it and remove the core then cut into thin slices. Season with a drizzle of oil, garlic and oregano.

9. All the pizza that has been stuffed to rest for 10 minutes and then bake in a static oven at 210 degrees or in a fan oven for 15 minutes.

10. You can now remove the marinara pizza from the oven and serve it hot.

Storage:

Marinara pizza can be frozen after half-cooked. When you want to eat it, finish cooking it in the oven or defrost it even at room temperature before serving.

Advice:

To spread the dough balls more easily, it is very important to allow them rest first.

Romana Pizza

Ingredients

- 600 ml water
- 7 g Dry brewer's yeast
- 1 kg 0 flour
- 60 g Extra virgin olive oil
- 20 g Salt

For the stuffing:
- 600 g Fiordilatte
- 10 g Oregano
- 700 g Tomato sauce
- 16 fillets Anchovies in oil
- 20 g Salt
- Extra virgin olive oil

Cook time: 15'
Preparation: 30'
Serves: 4
Cost: Low
Difficulty: Easy

Directions

1. In preparing Roman pizza, begin with the pizza dough. In a bowl, add the flour, 100 ml of water, yeast and use the planetary mixer with its hook mounted at medium-low speed.

2. Continue by adding water little at a time and make sure the flour has been well absorbed by water before adding more. Add salt and keep kneading after adding at least ¾ of water. Add the remaining water and allow the planetary mixer to work until you obtain a homogeneous and smooth mixture.

3. At this particular point, gradually add the oil little by little. Remove the dough from the planetary mixer when the oil has been fully absorbed and use your hands to shape it until you get a ball. Put the ball in a lightly greased bowl.

4. Use a clean cloth or a cling film to cover and allow it to rise in the oven while

lights are on. Hold on until the dough has doubled in its size but better if tripled and continue with the pizza preparation.

5. Transfer the dough to the pastry board once it rises and divide it in 4 equal parts. Do this for each of the balls. Let it stand for 30 minutes after covering it with a clean tea towel.

6. Use a drizzle of oil to lightly grease four 30 cm diameter pizza pans and put the dough ball in the center of the pan. Begin squeezing from the center outwards if necessary, pulling the sides slightly. If the dough tends to return to its original shape or it's too elastic, put aside the pizza that you spread and begin rolling another one, leave the previous one to rest. Try spreading the dough over the whole surface of the tray.

7. In a large bowl, pour in the tomato sauce and season with oil, pepper, salt and oregano. On the pizza base, pour a generous ladle of tomato sauce and spread it in a circular motion leaving only a boarder of 1.5 cm but covering almost the entire area.

8. Chop the mozzarella coarsely. Use a drizzle of oil, the mozzarella cut into small pieces and anchovy fillets to season the pizza. Allow the stuffed pizza to rest for 20 minutes and then bake it at 250 degrees in a static oven.

9. Serve your roman pizza immediately it is out of the oven.

Storage:

Roman-style pizza can be frozen after half-cooked. When you want to eat it, finish cooking it in the oven or defrost it even at room temperature before serving.

Advice:

If you realize that the mozzarella is very wet, squeeze it perfectly and allow it to drain on a colander before putting it on the pizza.

4 Cheeses Pizza

Ingredients

- 80 g Gorgonzola
- 500 g Bread dough
- 100 g Mozzarella
- 100 g Fontina
- 80 g Parmesan
- Salt to taste
- Pepper to taste
- 2 tbsp. Extra virgin olive oil
- 10 g 00 flour

Cook time: 25'
Preparation: 20'
Serves: 4
Cost: Low
Difficulty: Low

Directions

1. On a lightly floured pastry board, put the bread dough and roll it out using a rolling pin into a sheet of about 7 mm thick.
2. Brush a baking sheet with a drizzle of oil and on a cutting board, put the fontina and gorgonzola and remove the crust and cut them into small cubes using a sharp knife.
3. Chop the mozzarella coarsely and drain it. You could alternatively use some fiordilatte that has got a drier composition.
4. In the pan, spread all the cheese over the pasta and then flavor with a generous mince of pepper and a pinch of salt.
5. In a preheated oven at 220 degrees, bake the pizza for 25 minutes and then serve it while it's very hot.

4 Seasons Pizza

Cook time: 20'
Preparation: 40'
Serves: 4
Cost: Low
Difficulty: Easy

Ingredients

- 5 g Sugar
- 270 ml Water
- 500 g Manitoba flour
- 10 g Salt
- 50 ml Oil
- Extra virgin olive oil
- 500 ml Tomato sauce
- 10 g Salt
- 25 g Cube, fresh brewer's yeast
- Oregano
- 100 g Artichokes in oil
- 50 g Champignon mushrooms
- 120 g Cooked ham
- Mozzarella Cooking
- 50 g black olives

Directions

1. To prepare this type of pizza, begin with the dough. Get a bowl and pour in oil, water, sugar, salt and lastly the flour and yeast tube then begin kneading for about 20 minutes. Cover the dough with a cloth and allow it to rise for at least an hour in a dry and cool place that is away from the light.

2. Heat the oven to 200 degrees, and cut the mozzarella into thin slices and put it aside. In a bowl, pour in the tomato puree and use extra virgin olive oil, a pinch of salt and oregano to season it.

3. When the time for leavening ends, lay out the pasta after covering a baking sheet with parchment paper. Put the tomato puree on the top and then cook for 15 minutes in a preheated oven.

4. Clean and wash the artichokes, mushrooms and olives. Chop them finely and set them aside.

5. Remove the pizza from the oven after 15 minutes and arrange the mozzarella slices and divide the pizza into four wedges. In one wedge, arrange the chopped olives, in another wedge, arrange the champignon mushrooms, in the third wedge, arrange the artichokes and in the fourth and last wedge, put the cooked ham and bake for more 5 minutes.

6. Serve your 4 seasons pizza steaming and hot.

Tips:

In order to make a great 4 seasons pizza, it's advisable to allow the dough to rise well. Let it rise for a long time so that once your pizza is cooked, it will be fluffier and softer, do not rush to roll out the dough.

Another secret is how to lay the mozzarella. For the last five minutes of cooking, put the cut mozzarella in tubes and this will help in preventing the liquids that are produced by the mozzarella to wet the pizza base. Follow this same advice for the ham, mushrooms and artichokes. To avoid overcooking with the oven's high temperature, add the last few minutes of cooking.

To make your pizza more stenographic and embellish it, make sticks to be put on the surface with the dough that has been kept aside to divide it into wedges.

Siciliana Pizza

Cook time: 15'
Preparation: 6 h
Serves: 4
Cost: Low
Difficulty: Low

Ingredients

The dough:
- 250 g 00 flour
- ½ sachet dry brewer's yeast
- 250 g Remilled semolina
- 5 g Salt
- 2 spoons Olive oil
- 350 ml Water
- 1 tsp sugar

The dressing:
- Braid of Mozzarella
- Peeled tomatoes
- Oregano
- Basil
- Salt
- Anchovy fillets

Directions

1. In a bowl, put the yeast, sugar and flour and first mix. Add salt and water gradually, if the dough gets too hard, add more water and if it's soft, do not add the remaining water.
2. Lastly add the oil and begin using your hands to knead passing the dough on a pastry board. You can put the dough inside a planetary mixer if you have one and use a hook.
3. Take at least 10-15 minutes kneading the dough and when you get a soft but not sticky ball, allow it to rest for at least 3 hours after sprinkling it with flour.
4. Get a baking sheet and grease it. Roll out the dough on it and obtain a layer

that is not too high. Leave it to rise for another 3 hours.

5. Preheat the oven to maximum temperature. Season the tomato sauce with oregano, basil, oil and anchovy fillets, also stuff the well risen pizza and bake it for at least 10 minutes. Underneath, it should be golden brown.

6. Take the pizza out from the oven and fill the entire surface with crumbled mozzarella and then bake for more 5 minutes until the mozzarella melts.

7. Remove from the oven and before serving let it rest for at least 5 minutes.

Advice:

This particular dough is great with any filling type so you can leave the anchovy if you don't like it.

Diavola Pizza

Cook time: 10'
Preparation: 45'
Serves: 4
Cost: Low
Difficulty: Low

Ingredients

The dough:
- 200 ml Brewer's yeast
- ½ loaf
- 3 tbsp. Extra virgin olive oil
- 1 tsp salt
- 400 g 00 flour

The dressing:
- Extra virgin olive oil
- Salt to taste
- Oregano to taste
- 150 g Spicy salami
- 250 g Mozzarella
- 400 g Tomato sauce

Directions

1. 1. Start by preparing the pizza dough. Get a baking tray and grease it with a drizzle of oil, roll out the dough and put it there, cover with tomato puree and put the pizza to cook in an already hot oven for 10 minutes at 220 degrees.
2. 2. Meanwhile, slice the salami and cut the mozzarella into cubes. Remove the pizza from the oven and then evenly distribute the salami and mozzarella slices.
3. 3. Use a pinch of salt, drizzle of oil and a pinch of oregano to season and then continue cooking for other 20 minutes.

Ortolana Pizza

Ingredients

- 1 Yellow pepper
- Pepper to taste
- 1 tbsp. dried oregano
- 200 g Mozzarella
- 50 g Black olives
- 1 egg plant
- 3 tbsp. extra virgin olive oil
- 2 Courgettes
- Salt to taste
- 400 g Bread dough
- 30 g Caper in salt
- 200 g tomato puree

Cook time: 25'
Preparation: 30'
Serves: 4
Cost: Low
Difficulty: Easy

Directions

1. Start by cleaning the courgettes and aubergine. Peel and cut them into slices about half a centimeter thick lengthwise and allow them grill under a grill in the oven or a cast iron.
2. Peel the peppers and put them in the prongs of a fork one at a time. Cut them into strips after peeling them and toast them on the flame.
3. In boiling water, blanch the tomato, allow it to dry, then peel it and cut it into strips. Cut into strips the grilled aubergine. Use oil to grease a round pizza pan.
4. On the bottom, spread the bread dough and use your fingers to flatten it and with the fork prongs, prick it here and there.
5. In a bowl, put all vegetables with a pinch of salt, teaspoon of oil, half

teaspoon of oregano and a pinch of pepper and allow them to steep for 10 minutes.

6. Spread the vegetables over pasta and sprinkle them with basil strips and diced mozzarella. Use the remaining oil to sprinkle.

Napoletana Pizza

Ingredients

- 600 g Water
- 7 g Dry brewer's yeast
- 60 g Extra virgin olive oil
- 20 g Salt
- 1 kg 0 Flour
- 20 g Salt

To season:
- 24 Caper fruits
- 16 fillets Anchovies in oil
- Extra virgin olive oil
- 700 g Tomato sauce
- 10 g Oregano
- Black pepper to taste
- 20 g Salt

Cook time: 15'
Preparation: 30'
Serves: 4
Cost: Low
Difficulty: Medium
Rising time: 4 h

Directions

1. To make the napoletana pizza, begin by pouring the flour into a mixer bowl. Add 100 ml of water and yeast and then use a hook mounted at medium-low speed to operate the planetary mixer.

2. Continue by adding water little at a time and make sure you wait till the previous dose is well absorbed by the flour. When you have added at least ¾ of water, keep kneading after adding salt. Always keep adding the rest of the water flush and allow it to work until you get a homogeneous and smooth mixture.

3. Gradually add the oil at this point and remove the dough from the planetary mixer once the oil has absorbed completely and use your hands to shape it

until you form a ball. Put it in a bowl that is lightly greased.

4. Use a clean cloth or a cling film to cover and allow it to rise in the oven while lights are on. Hold on until the dough has doubled in its size but better if tripled and continue with the pizza preparation.

5. Transfer the dough to the pastry board once it rises and divide it in 4 equal parts. Do this for each of the balls. Let it stand for 30 minutes after covering it with a clean tea towel.

6. Use a drizzle of oil to lightly grease four 30 cm diameter pizza pans and put the dough ball in the center of the pan. Begin squeezing from the center outwards if necessary, pulling the sides slightly. If the dough tends to return to its original shape or it's too elastic, put aside the pizza that you spread and begin rolling another one, leave the previous one to rest. Try spreading the dough over the whole surface of the tray.

7. In a large bowl, pour in the tomato sauce and season with oil, pepper, salt and oregano. On the pizza base, pour a generous ladle of tomato sauce and spread it in a circular motion leaving only a boarder of 1.5 cm but covering almost the entire area. Set the caper fruits aside after cutting them in half.

8. You can now do the seasoning with caper fruits cut into half, a drizzle of oil and anchovies. Allow the pizza that has been stuffed to rest for 10 minutes and use a static oven to bake for 20 minutes at 210 degrees.

9. Serve the Napoletana pizza as soon as you remove it from the oven.

Storage:

Napoletana pizza can be frozen after half-cooked. When you want to eat it, finish cooking it in the oven or defrost it even at room temperature before serving.

Advice:

Remember to wash the salted capers very well under running water if you are to use them and before putting them on the pizza, slightly dry them.

Tuna and Onions Pizza

Ingredients

- 350 g 00 flour
- 350 g Durum wheat flour
- Pizza dough
- 10-15 g Salt
- Olive oil to taste
- 550-600 ml Lukewarm water
- 1-2 g Fresh brewer's yeast

To season:
- 1 red onion
- 100 ml Tomato sauce
- 200 g Mozzarella
- 160 g Tuna in oil
- Black olives
- Green olives in brine
- Cherry tomatoes

- Oregano to taste

Cook time: 20'
Preparation: 20'
Serves: 2
Cost: Low
Difficulty: Low

Directions

To prepare this soft pizza, you make a very soft dough using 1 g of brewer's yeast with leavening at room temperature and if in winter, it will need at least 15-18 hours and in the heat like 4-7 hours.

Dissolve the brewer's yeast in 150 ml of warm water. Mix the two flours in a bowl, then add salt and mix very well. Make a hole in the center and put the yeast with the water too and again add more water like 450 ml and the remaining water, we'll add as we work on the ingredients.

Use a fork to miss the water and flour and when you realize that the dough is getting harder, add 50 ml more of water and continue that way until you get a soft mixture that has been worked on using a fork. You actually don't need to knead using your hands.

Continue using a fork to turn until the dough is tied. This will take only few minutes. Then leave in the heat to rise for at least 4 hours or little more time.

Once the dough is well leavened, you will realize that it forms bubbles, then get to prepare the onion and soft tuna pizzas.

Use olive oil to grease the oven plate or 2 pizza pans. Divide the dough in 2 parts or leave it whole. Pour some little oil on the dough and spread it all over the pan. Since it is very soft dough, it will take a moment and won't stick to the pan or on hands and contrary during the cooking process, it forms a base golden crust, which is delicious, and this makes the pizza in the pan unique.

When the dough is stretched out in the pan, we go to the part of seasoning. Begin with slicing the onions into slices. Red onion is recommended and also spread the passata on the dough.

Cut the mozzarella into small pieces, slice the onions and add, add the tuna in olive oil as well.

In the oven cook one pizza at a time at maximum temperature of 230 degrees in an oven fan. Cook until the edges become golden brown and this takes at least 20 minutes.

Remove it from the oven and serve.

Capricciosa Pizza

Ingredients

- 1 tbsp. Olive oil
- 1 pinch, Chopped dry oregano
- 230-250 g Pizza dough
- 30 g Sliced cooked ham
- 150 g Tomato sauce
- 40 g Sliced black and green olives
- 4-5 Well drained anchovies in oil
- 50 g Mozzarella for pizza
- Fresh basil leaves
- 40 g Artichokes in oil, drained
- 30 g fresh champignon mushrooms, sliced
- Salt to taste

Cook time: 20'
Preparation: 30'
Serves: 1
Cost: Low
Difficulty: Medium

Directions

1. Prepare and spread the dough you prefer and then mix in a pinch of dried oregano, chopped, anchovies chopped and well drained, a pinch of salt, teaspoon of olive oil and 150 g of tomato puree and flavor the pizza base using this sauce.

2. On the pizza, add other ingredients by haphazardly spreading them, that is 30 g of sliced and cooked ham, 30 g of champignon mushrooms sliced, 40 g of green and black olives, 50 g of mozzarella for pizza and 40 g of artichokes that are in oil, drained and cut into pieces.

3. Take back the seasoned pizza to the oven that was preheated at 250 degrees while the grill is on and allow it to cook for 15-20 minutes until it's cooked

completely, the mozzarella melts, the dough edges turn to golden brown and the pizza bottom turns out dry nicely.

4. Depending on the ingredient's quality, type and thickness of the dough used and oven type, cooking times vary since every oven even cooks differently.

5. Take out the capricciosa pizza once it has been cooked and then garnish it with few fresh basil leaves and then serve immediately.

Seafood Pizza

Ingredients

For the dough:
- 300 ml water
- 30 g Extra virgin olive oil
- 1 tsp Barley malt
- 50 g Flour
- 8 g Salt
- 20 g Brewer's yeast

For the filling:
- 300 g Prawns
- 300 g Mussels
- 200 g Tomato sauce
- 500 g Clams
- Extra virgin olive oil
- Salt to taste
- 1 Sprig Parsley

Cook time: 20'
Preparation: 40'
Serves: 2
Cost: Low
Difficulty: Low

Directions

1. In preparing the seafood pizza, begin by preparing the pizza dough. In a bowl, put the salt, malt and flour, you can alternatively use sugar. Mix the ingredients and then add the water at room temperature where you will have dissolved the brewer's yeast. Add some oil and then work on everything until you get elastic and smooth dough.

2. Use the dough to form a ball and put it in a bowl to rise. Use a plastic wrap to cover it and keep it in a warm place until it doubles or for at least 4 hours.

3. Get the dough and divide it in two parts. From it, form two loaves and allow them to rest on a floured surface for 1 hour at room temperature. You can use

a cloth to cover in order to avoid power surges.

4. To form a sheet, the size of a pan, roll out each loaf and then put them in greased trays. Over the pizzas, spread a layer of tomato puree, drizzle with a drizzle of oil, season with salt and bake for 8 minutes in a preheated oven at 200 degrees.

5. Remove the pizzas from the oven and then distribute the seafood i.e. the raw prawns, the mussels and clams that were previously cooked and then bake for other 5 minutes and make sure the seafood doesn't dry out.

6. Distribute a little chopped fresh parsley after removing from the oven. Your seafood is now ready. Serve.

Sea and Mountains Pizza

Ingredients

- Flour
- Olive oil
- 500 g bread dough
- 1 tbsp. parsley
- Garlic to taste
- 5 Pear tomato
- White wine to taste
- 1 kg mussel
- Butter to taste
- Salt and pepper to taste
- 5 kg mushrooms, dried

Cook time: 40'
Preparation: 20'
Serves: 4
Cost: Low
Difficulty: Easy

Directions

1. In preparing the seafood pizza, begin by preparing the pizza dough. In a 1. Under running water, scrape 1 kg of mussels and in a covered saucepan on high flame, leave them to open. Remove shells for 3 quarters and leave the rest kept in their shells.

2. 2. Clean at least 500 g of fresh mushrooms and then cut them into slices.

3. 3. In a large saucepan, put 10 g of butter and 3 tablespoons of oil and brown 3 garlic cloves. Add the pepper, salt and mushrooms. On low heat, cover them and sauté for 5-6 minutes.

4. 4. Use 1 teaspoon of flour and 1 tablespoon of chopped parsley to sprinkle. Also use half a glass of wine to sprinkle and turn off the heat after thickening over low heat.

5. 5. On the oven plate greased with oil, spread 500 g of bread dough. Spread at least 5 Perini tomatoes cut into rounds over the pasta. Put in a hot oven to

cook for 15 minutes at 200 degrees after sprinkling with some little salt and oil.

6. 6. Take the plate away from the oven and put all the mussels on tomatoes. Put in the oven to bake for 10 minutes at 210 degrees while they are covered with the mushrooms.

Ham and Mushrooms Pizza

Ingredients

- 200 g Mushrooms in oil
- 300 g Tomato sauce
- 600 g Bread dough
- 250 g Mozzarella
- Basil
- 100 ml Extra virgin olive oil
- Garlic to taste
- Salt and Pepper To Taste
- 150 g Baked Ham

Cook time: 20'
Preparation: 10'
Serves: 4
Cost: Low
Difficulty: Medium

Directions

1. In preparing the ham and mushroom pizza, take 1 tablespoon of extra virgin olive oil and bread dough. On a floured work surface, roll it and make a sheet of 1 cm thickness.

2. On the pizza, put the tomato puree and add the clean and well-chopped garlic.

3. Then cut into strips the baked ham and then sprinkle on the whole pizza.

4. Lastly add the mozzarella tubes and in oil, add the mushrooms. Season with pepper and extra virgin olive oil.

5. Put it in a hot oven to bake at 250 degrees for about 15 minutes.

6. Serve the ham and mushroom pizza while hot.

Apulian Pizza

Cook time: 1h 30'
Preparation: 20'
Serves: 4
Cost: Low
Difficulty: Easy

Ingredients

- QB flour
- Extra virgin olive oil
- 2 onions
- 4 Anchovies in oil
- 10 Pitted black olives
- 1 bunch of basil
- 4 tbsp. tomato puree
- Salt to taste
- 400 g Pizza dough
- 12 Cherry tomatoes

Directions

1. For 40 minutes, boil the potatoes in their skins. Using a special utensil, peel and mash them and make them fall on the pastry board.

2. Mix the potatoes with a pinch of salt, flour and yeast dissolved in 2 tablespoons of warm water. Work on it well until you get a soft paste. If possible, add lukewarm water.

3. Meanwhile, in boiling water, blanch the tomatoes and peel them. Free them from seeds and cut them into small pieces. You can a well cut the mozzarella into slices.

4. Get 1 26 cm diameter round mold and grease it, use the dough to cover the bottom and make a layer to tomato slices and mozzarella over it.

5. Season with a pinch of salt and oregano and use grated cheese to season. Use oil to drizzle and allow it to rise for at least 1 hour.

6. In a hot oven set at 170 degrees, put the pizza and allow it to cook for 30 minutes then serve it hot.

Tyrolean Pizza

Ingredients

For the pizza:
- 1 tsp Sugar
- 12 g Brewer's yeast
- 500 g 00 flour
- 3 tbsp. Extra virgin olive oil
- 250-300 ml Warmed water
- 2 tsps Salt

For the dressing:
- Fresh ground oregano to taste
- 1 Medium golden onion
- 1 tsp sugar
- 250 g Tomato sauce
- 400 g Mozzarella, well drained
- 250 g Speck, cut into thin slices
- 2 packs of pork frankfurters

Cook time: 15'
Preparation: 30'
Serves: 4
Cost: Low
Difficulty: Easy

Directions

Classic Mixture

1. On a pastry board, arrange the flour and give it a shape of the classic fountain.
2. On the outermost edge of the flour, that where you should put the salt.
3. Smash the brewer's yeast and dissolve it in 100 ml of warm water together with the sugar. Pour the mixture in the center of the fountain after adding

the oil.

4. Use your fingertips to begin working on the dough. Incorporate the flour gradually to the fountain edge. Add the necessary lukewarm water gradually and in a circular motion.

5. From the edge, include more and more flour until elastic, soft and smooth dough forms at the center.

6. On a floured surface, vigorously work on the dough until it doesn't stick on your hands anymore.

Mixture with the Planetary Mixer

1. In a planetary mixer with a mounted hook, insert the flour and add yeast, oil and 150 ml of water.

2. At medium-low speed, knead for 5 minutes and also adding the rest of the water flush.

3. Again, knead for 5 minutes, add salt and keep cooking for more 5 minutes until you obtain elastic, smooth and homogenous dough.

How to make Tyrolean Pizza

1. Form a ball with the dough that has been prepared using a planetary mixer or by hand and use a cloth to cover after making a cross cut.

2. In a draft free and warm place, leave the dough to rise until it doubles in volume for about 2 hours

3. Divide the dough into 4 loaves once its volume doubles and put them in a container with a well-floured container, with a lid.

4. Allow the dough to rise. This takes a couple of hours then go to the pizza preparation, one at a time.

5. Sprinkle the first loaf with flour and put it on a lightly greased round pan. For beginners, you can use a drizzle of oil to first moisten the fingertips.

6. Lightly press on the dough using your fingers so as to give it a circular shape.

7. Make a movement that goes from the center to the edge when handling the

pizza so as to push the gas bubbles, which are formed after the rising process towards the cornice. You should not flatten the latter as it must be crisp and high at the end of the cooking.

8. Before baking the pizzas, preheat the oven for 30 minutes at 250 degrees. Then go to preparing the seasoning, which will be divided in 4 portions. Slice the onions thinly after peeling and rinsing them.

9. For 2 minutes, blanch the frankfurters and then cut them in thin slices. In a bowl, put the tomato sauce and do the seasoning with 2 tablespoons of oregano, salt, pepper and oil and also cut the mozzarella into long slices that are thin.

10. Spread ¼ of the tomato sauce for the first pizza using the back of a spoon. In succession, distribute the frankfurters, onions and mozzarella.

11. Use oil to wet the pizza surface and place it in an already hot oven. Since the pizza must cook more below than above, put the pan near the oven bottom.

12. Allow the Tyrolean pizza to cook until the cornice has become golden and crispy and the pizza bottom is dry. This will take 13-15 minutes. Raise the bottom to see if the pizza is cooked.

13. Remove the Tyrolean pizza from the oven when it finishes cooking, transfer it to a plate and then use speck slices to garnish it.

14. You can now serve the freshly baked Tyrolean pizza.

Boscaiola Pizza

Cook time: 15'
Preparation: 10'
Serves: 4
Cost: Low
Difficulty: Low

Ingredients

- 200 g Sausage
- 130 g Mozzarella
- Extra virgin olive oil to taste
- 400 g Pizza dough
- Black pepper to taste
- 150 g Champignon mushrooms
- Salt to taste

Directions

1. Begin with preparing the pizza dough. Leave the dough to rise as you take care of the rest of the things. Clean and then cut the mushrooms into thin slices and then do the seasoning with pepper and a pinch of salt.

2. Grease a 30 cm pan with a drizzle of oil to avoid the pizza from sticking and dice the mozzarella.

3. Spread the dough in the pan directly once it is ready using your hands. Sprinkle with slices of champignon and diced mozzarella. Lastly, lay the sausage that is crumbled in small pieces and if desired, sprinkle with other oil.

4. Preheat a static oven at 250 degrees and put the dough for 12-15 minutes. It is recommended to put the pan in the lower part of the oven and not in the center exactly and also check the times according to the appliance you are using.

5. Take the boscaiola pizza out, cut and serve it. You can also accompany it with a nice beer.

Storage:

6. You can choose to leave the pizza in the refrigerator and, if necessary, reheat it. After cooking and letting it cool, you can also freeze it.

Calzone

Cook time: 10'
Preparation: 40'
Serves: 6
Cost: Low
Difficulty: Medium

Ingredients

- 500 g 0 flour
- 25 g Brewer's yeast, Fresh
- 300 ml water
- 1 tsp Sugar
- 30 g Extra virgin olive oil
- 10 g Salt

For the classic filling:
- 60 g Ham, cooked
- 10 g Extra virgin olive oil
- 60 g Mozzarella
- 100 g Tomato puree
- Salt to taste

Ingredients for the vegetarian filling:
- 50 g Courgettes
- 50 g Red peppers
- 60 g Mozzarella
- 50 g Carrots
- 50 g Eggplants
- Black pepper to taste
- 10 g Extra virgin olive oil
- Salt to taste

Directions

1. Begin with dough preparation following the procedure. In a warm and dry place, allow it to rise for at least 2 hours until the dough doubles.

2. When the dough rises, begin the preparation of vegetables filling through washing and shredding them finely in various vegetable varieties like pepper, carrots, aubergines and zucchini.

3. In a pan, put a spoonful of oil, salt and pepper and on high heat, sauté them for few minutes. On the colander, put the mozzarella that has been cut into cubes for it to lose the excess water.

4. Cut the mozzarella well into cubes, drain it very well and then ham into small pieces. Use oil, 100 ml of tomato sauce and salt to do the seasoning, this is for the classic filling.

5. On a work surface, roll out the dough high 2mm and 18 cm wide rectangles; put the filling in small piles that are arranged in the rectangle center.

6. On one side, lift the dough and cover the overlapping filling on the other side. Use a glass or 10 cm diameter pastry cutter and cut half-moon breeches and use the fork edges to press on the side to be glued.

7. Use oil to lightly brush the mini shoes and in a fan, oven heated at 230 degrees, bake for 10 to 15 minutes.

8. These mini-baked shoes will be served hot but be very careful and not burn yourself with the filling.

Chapter 5: Special Pizzas

Fried Pizza

Ingredients

- 2 g Dry brewer's yeast
- 500 g Manitoba flour
- 10 g Salt
- 320 g Water

For the stuffing:
- 100 g Provola
- 8 Basil leaves
- 300 g Buffalo Ricotta
- 60 g Salami
- 200 g Peeled tomatoes
- Black pepper to taste
- Salt to taste

For frying:
- Seed oil

Cook time: 10'
Preparation: 30'
Serves: 4
Cost: Low
Difficulty: Medium

Directions

1. Into a planetary with a hook, add dry beer yeast and sifted flour. Add 80 g water and use the mixer to mix. Little by little, add water into the mixer and ensure that it is absorbed. When ¾ of the water is added, pour salt and keep kneading.

2. Pour in the water that remained, flush, and keeping working on it till the hook is strung by the dough and it is homogeneously smooth. Remove the dough and place on a flour-dusted work surface.

3. Use your hands to spread the dough and fold in the flaps from the edges towards the middle.

4. Form the dough into a sphere and move it to a big bowl and use a plastic

wrap to cover. Put it in the oven for 3 hours at a temperature of 25-28 ° to let it rise.

5. Transfer the dough to a pastry board dusted with flour. Form into loaf and then divide it using a tarot into for equal parts.

6. Form each part into balls and arrange them spacing them. Use a non-stretched film to cover the balls and put in a turned-off oven with light on again for 3 hours for it to rise.

7. In the meantime, get the filling ready: cube the provola and the salami. Also, prepare ricotta and basil leaves: make it creamier by using a spoon to work on it.

8. After 3 hours, use your hands to spread the balls on a pastry board and form a disc of an irregular shape of diameter of about 30 cm.

9. Work on the filling now: use just a ¼ of the ingredients for every pizza leaving a few cm from the edges. Using a fork spread the ricotta and the tomatoes.

10. Add Provola and salami cubes to taste. Add chopped basil leaves. Fold over the part unfilled to form a half moon. Repeat until all pizzas are made and then start cooking.

11. Add some oil to a pan and ensure the temperature reaches 170 °. Fry a pizza at a time. Add some hot oil as you cook to cover the pizza. Turn to cook the other side until it is gold in color.

12. Use a slotted pain to drain pizza and put it to dry on an absorbent paper.

Storage

The pizza dough can be stored in a refrigerated up to 24 hours but it should be covered with a cling film. You can also freeze it.

Gluten-Free Pizza

Ingredients

- 1 tsp Honey
- 350 g Rice flour
- 250 g Corn starch
- 2 tbsp. Extra virgin olive oil
- 10 g Salt
- 25 g Fresh brewer's yeast
- 350 ml Water

To season:

- 2 tbsp. Extra virgin olive oil
- 350 ml Tomato sauce
- 500 g Fiordilatte mozzarella
- Basil to taste
- Oregano to taste
- Salt to taste

To grease the trays:

- Extra virgin olive oil to taste

Cook time: 15'
Preparation: 30'
Serves: 2
Cost: Very Low
Difficulty: Easy

Directions

1. Sift the cornstarch and flour and pour them on a pastry board. Form a hole at the middle. Add in a glass of brewer's yeast, honey and warm water and oil. Combine by stir until everything is dissolved.

2. On a separate bowl, add a glass of warm water and dissolve some salt and add oil. Combine with the flour mixture.

3. Add the water and oil mixture. Knead using a mixer or your hand. Add water and flour accordingly in order to make smooth dough. Integrate until you

form homogenous dough, which is smooth. Form 8 balls and place on a flour dusted bowl. Use a clean tea towel to cover the dough and put it an oven switched off for an oven. Season with oregano, salt or oil and go on to make the pizza dough.

4. Grease a pan and roll the dough on the pan. Brush some oil on the pizza's oil and allow 1 hour for it to rise. When it is leavened, drizzle tomato puree, olive oil on the pizza and bake for 10 minutes in a preheated oven at 200 °. In the meantime, slice the mozzarella and add to the colander so as to remove the conservation water. Remove pizza and add some mozzarella and let rest for 5 more minutes. Remove the pizza from the oven, add some fresh basil leaves and serve right away

Pizza and Mortazza

Ingredients

- 300 g Water, at room temperature
- 2 g Dry brewer's yeast
- 460 g 0 Flour
- 50 g Extra virgin olive oil
- 10 g Salt
- 5 g Sugar

For seasoning and stuffing:
- Extra virgin olive oil to taste
- 300 g Mortadella, sliced
- Coarse salt to taste

Cook time: 20'
Preparation: 30'
Serves: 6
Cost: Very Low
Difficulty: Difficult

Directions

1. In preparing the pizza and mortazza, begin with the pizza dough. Using your hands or a planetary mixer with a hook, pour in the sifted flour. Add the granulated sugar and dehydrated yeast. If you choose to use your hands, it takes much time for the dough to be homogeneous and smooth.

2. Begin by working on the powders and then pour in the lukewarm water gradually and pour in the olive oil once it is absorbed. Continue using a hook to work on it until you get homogenous dough and lastly add the salt.

3. Stop the planetary mixer after kneading the dough for at least 15 minutes. The dough will be very soft and hydrated. Oil the work surface with about 5 g of oil at this point and in order to work on the dough very well, grease your hands well.

4. Transfer the pizza dough on the oiled worktop and use your hands to work on it for few minutes and make creases.

5. Pull and fold the dough edges inward. This is done in order to make such

dough types more elastic, very hydrated and workable. If it's possible, let the dough rest for few minutes at each fold and cover it with a cling film and then start making the folds again.

6. Use the dough to form a ball and put it in a bowl and use a plastic wrap to cover it. Leave it in the oven to rise for about 3 hours with the lights on at a maximum temperature of 28-30 degrees. The dough must double in its volume. The dough will be transferred to the refrigerator and allow it to rise overnight.

7. Take the dough out of the fridge the next day and bring it to room temperature for at least 1 hour. It won't be cold when you pick it up. Use at least 20 g of oil to oil the bottom of a 35x28 cm rectangular tray and turn the dough directly into the tray upside down.

8. Use your hands to spread it and make sure it extends and covers the whole surface. Let the pizza rise again for 30-60 minutes once finished and sprinkle the coarse salt over the entire surface and also season with 10 g of extra virgin olive oil.

9. In a preheated static oven, cook the pizza for 20 minutes at 220 degrees. The pizza must be crunchier at the base and soft on the top. You can put the pan in the lower part of the oven if you have a gas oven. If you want to get a result closer to the original roman pizza, you can heat the pan you want to use for cooking minus oiling it until it becomes very hot and lay the dough with a spatula and on the shovel, spread by hand.

10. Take the pizza out of the oven once cooked and allow it to cool. Divide it in six parts and divide each part in a half. Fill every portion with slices of mortadella and serve the pizza for a yummy savory snack.

Storage:

It's advisable to consume stuffed pizza and mortazza freshly. Unfilled pizza can be kept in a paper bag for 1 day and heated slightly before stuffing.

Advice:

Your pizza will be crunchier at the base if you are in possession of a refractory stone. In an oven, heat the stone for at least 30 minutes and put the dough that has already been spread using a shovel.

Fried Pizzelle

Ingredients

- 4 g Fresh brewer's yeast
- 700 g 00 flour
- 20 g Salt
- 500 ml water at room temperature

To season the pizzelle:
- 25 Basil leaves
- Oregano to taste
- 720 g San Marzano peeled tomatoes
- 1 garlic clove
- Extra virgin olive oil to taste
- 70 g Grana Padano DOP to be grated
- Salt to taste

For frying
- Peanut oil

Cook time: 25'
Preparation: 40'
Serves: 25
Cost: Medium
Difficulty: Difficult
Rising time: 6 h

Directions

1. To make the fried pizzelle, begin by making the dough. In a small jug, pour in an indicated amount of water at room temperature, add the fresh crumbled brewer's yeast and use a teaspoon to stir until it's dissolved completely.

2. In the meantime, leave the yeast to rest and on one side of the cupboard, put about 30% of the flour, which withstands the dough temperature well and keeps it from not sticking to the edges. You can as well use a glass bowl or a wooden container. Pour the water in the other half of the cupboard and avoid pouring it on the flour directly.

3. In the water, add the salt and mix gently with your hands to dissolve it. Start mixing the flour as long as you don't hear any grain any longer.

4. Use your hands gradually making a rotating movement to mix the water and the flour. Add the previously dissolved yeast to the dough after putting at least 50% of the flour dose. Keep kneading and also adding more flour until it has incorporated fully. Using hands to make the dough allow you to adjust the dough consistency better and know if you require adding more flour.

5. At this point, keep working inside the bowl or cupboard for 10-15 minutes until it is homogeneous and smooth. Allow the dough to rise inside the cupboard and use a clean and slightly moistened cloth to cover it. It should rise in a place protected from sudden hot-cold temperature changes or drafts.

6. At room temperature, allow it to rise away from drafts for at least 4 hours. Use a tarot to transfer the dough at this time to a lightly floured surface. Divide them into 50 g portions by use of a tarot and with these doses, you will then get like 25 portions.

7. Using a little flour, form balls by giving each portion of the folds putting the flaps under and put them on a lightly floured tray gradually.

8. Use a dry cloth to cover and let it rest in a place away from drafts for at least 2 hours.

9. Meanwhile, take care of the sauce. To a glass bowl, transfer the San Marzano tomatoes and use your hands to fray them. You can use a fork as an alternative. Into a pan, pour a drizzle of oil and the previously crushed garlic cloves and allow it to fry until golden brown and then eliminate them.

10. In a pan, add the tomato and then do the seasoning with salt. On low heat, add the oregano and let it cook for at least 30 minutes until it shrinks. Keep turning is as you cook.

11. Put a large saucepan with peanut butter on the fire after the 2 hours of leavening to bring to a maximum temperature of 180 degrees. Using a tarot, help detaching from the tray a portion at a time and take it to the work surface, which is slightly floured.

12. Roll out your first pizzella and gently spread it using your fingertips. Lightly prick the dough using the tarot tip, this helps it not to swell too much during cooking. Immerse the pizzella as soon as the oil reaches the temperature indicated and use a spoon to crush it in the center to create a central cavity which once the pizzella is cooked will be collected to contain the seasoning and to also prevent the excessive swelling.
13. Drain the pizzella with a sciumarola when it becomes golden brown and put it on a sheet of fried paper. Keep cooking all the others and once they are all cooked, season them. Into the cavity of every pizzella, you can pour in a little grated cheese and a spoonful of tomato sauce.
14. End with the fresh basil leaves and then serve your pizzelle while still hot.

Storage:

It's recommended to consume the pizzelle while it's still hot.

You can alternatively refrigerate the dough for 1-day maximum or, before the second rising, you can freeze it.

Advice:

Fried pizzelle are yummy snacks and if you prefer to make them tastier, add a sprinkle of grated salted ricotta, an anchovy fillet or some Gaeta olives.

Red Pizzas

Cook time: 15'

Preparation: 25'

Serves: 24

Cost: Low

Difficulty: Medium

Note: Leavening 3h

Ingredients

- 500 g 00 flour
- 10 g Fresh brewer's yeast
- 12 g Sugar
- 250 g Water at room temperature
- 15 g Salt
- 60 g Extra virgin olive oil

For the dressing:
- 250 g mozzarella
- 1 tsp Salt
- 350 g Tomato sauce
- 2 tbsp. Extra virgin olive oil
- 2 tbsp. Oregano
- Black pepper to taste

Directions

1. To make red pizzas, begin by pouring flour in a bowl, add yeast and water. Use a wooden spoon to mix. Then add salt, oil and sugar.

2. To incorporate the ingredients, stir and then transfer to a working surface and vigorously mix until all is smooth.

3. With the worked dough, form a sphere, put oil in a large bowl and put the dough there. Use a cling film to cover and leave it for 3 hours at room temperature to rise in an oven that is turned off but lights are on and also away from the drafts. When the leavening hours elapse, the dough will have tripled in volume.

4. Meanwhile, take care of the pizza dressing. Pour the tomatoes in a bowl and season with pepper, salt, oil and oregano. Use a spoon to mix everything and

keep them aside until the time you need to use them.

5. Onto the pastry board, transfer the dough that was leavened and use very little flour to sprinkle. Use a rolling pin to roll out and obtain a rectangle of about 4 mm thick.

6. Oil the dripping pan where you will cook the pizza thoroughly. Couple the dough using a 7.5 diameter 19 cm pastry ring. Give a spherical shape to the redundant dough and allow it to rest for about 10 minutes.

7. You can knead again the excess and get 24 pizzas in all. Use a tarot to take them one by one and begin placing them on the oiled pan.

8. Form a small bowl in the center once arranged and at the edge leave about 0.5 cm. Cut the mozzarella into cubes and use the diced mozzarella and tomatoes to season in the center. Use a pinch of oregano and drizzle of oil.

9. In a static oven preheated at 200 degrees, bake the pizzas and for the first 10 minutes, cook positioning the pan at the oven base and the remaining minutes on the top shelf.

10. Once your red pizza is cooked, take it out of the oven and serve hot.

Storage:

It's recommended to consume the red pizzas as soon as they are ready or are heated slightly because they are good when hot.

The dough can be frozen once is has risen. But it's much better if it's already divided in portions and kept in a frost bag. It becomes sufficient to thaw the portion at room temperature and continue per the recipe.

You can freeze the pizzas from cooked seeds if you prefer, cook then half and allow them to cool, then cover with aluminum foil and freeze them at a temperature slightly lower than the one indicated in the recipe.

Advice:

You can make large red pizzas if you want. For example, you can get about 18 pizzas if you use a 9 cm pastry cutter. Add seasonings according to your taste

Pizza Roll

Ingredients

- 250 g 00 flour
- 2 g Dry brewer's yeast
- 155 g Water at room temperature
- 5 g Salt
- 5 g Malt
- 10 g Extra virgin olive oil

For the stuffing:
- 150 g Tomato sauce
- 100 g Cooked ham thinly sliced
- 150 g Mozzarella fior di latte
- 10 g Basil

To brush
- 10 g Extra virgin olive oil

Cook time: 40'
Preparation: 30'
Serves: 4
Cost: Low
Difficulty: Low

Rising time: 3h

Directions

1. In making the stuffed pizza roll, begin by making the basic dough. Into a bowl, pour in the water at room temperature add salt and use a spoon to mix in order to dissolve it, pour in extra virgin olive oil and mix the emulsion again.

2. Sift the flour in another large bowl, then add half the water mixture, salt, oil, dehydrated beer yeast and malt. Begin using your hands to knead or you can also use a fork. Keep the remaining emulsion and little flour close to you which you will gradually integrate in the dough to get the consistency you desire which must be elastic and soft basing on the flour you have used, it may take less or little more water.

3. On a surface, keep kneading until you get a soft, smooth but consistent dough that you will use to form a ball. Leave it in the bowl and use a plastic

wrap to cover. Leave it in the oven with lights on but when it is turned off and let the dough rise and double in the size and volume. You will need a temperature between 26-30 degrees and about 2-3 hours.

4. Meanwhile, prepare the filling ingredients. Into a bowl, pour in the tomato sauce and use basil leaves chopped with your hands, extra virgin olive oil, and salt to season.

5. Cut the mozzarella into cubes and put it in a colander to drain. It's crucial for it to dry to avoid it loosing liquids by moistening the dough during cooking.

6. Take the dough that has doubled in volume once the leavening period is over and take it on a lightly floured pastry board. Use a rolling pin to roll out until you get a sheet that is oval shaped measuring 38x34 cm.

7. On the pastry, sprinkle the tomato sauce and make sure to leave some centimeters from the edge. Cover the fresh basil leaves with diced mozzarella and lastly lay the cooked ham slices.

8. Use oil to brush the edges left to make the roll adhere well when closed. Inwardly close the edges so that they fall on the filling part and avoid the filling from coming out during the cooking.

9. Roll the dough from the longest side at this point and transfer the roll onto the dripping pan that is lined with parchment paper and seal the ends.

10. Use olive oil to brush the surface and bake for 40 minutes in a preheated static oven at 180 degrees.

11. Remove your stuffed pizza roll from the oven and allow it to rest for at least 10 minutes before cutting it into 27 slices.

Storage:

Your stuffed pizza roll can be stored in a refrigerator for 1 day and then heat it up when you serve it.

If you have used all the fresh ingredients, you can alternatively cook it half way and then freeze it in order to finish the cooking in the oven as it's required.

Advice:

You can prepare the dough the night before and leave it in the fridge overnight. It will be sufficient to leave it at room temperature for a couple of hours the following day before spreading it. Try stuffing your pizza roll with grilled vegetables or different cold cuts.

Fried Pizza with Mortadella and Fiordilatte

Ingredients

- 3 g Fresh brewer's yeast
- 415 g 00 flour
- 250 g Water
- 15 g Salt
- For the stuffing:
- 70 g Water
- 120 g Mortadella thick slices
- 220 g Fiordilatte
- Black pepper to taste
- 350 g Buffalo ricotta
- Basil to taste
- For frying:
- Peanut oil

Cook time: 5'
Preparation: 40'
Serves: 4
Cost: Medium
Difficulty: Difficult
Rising time: 8 h

Directions

1. To make the fried pizza with mortadella and fiordilatte, in a large bowl, put the required amount of water, add the brewer's yeast and use your hands to dissolve it.

2. In a bowl, sift the flour, add the salt and use the back of a wooden spoon to mix. Add almost half the flour and use a spoon to stir until you obtain a batter. Carry out all these operations in order to respect the absorption times of the flour.

3. At intervals, add the remaining flour and you will be able to regulate the amount you add better and the dough will become softer. After using a wooden spoon to incorporate all the flour that is necessary, start using your hands to knead inside the bowl by collecting the flour on the inside edges of

the bowl and bringing the dough inwards.

4. Transfer the dough to a work surface when the container is clean. It will already have its compactness though it will still be raw. Add a flour veil and for 2-3 minutes, make the folds by adding more flour. The dough shouldn't be too smooth.

5. Keep working by closing the dough in this way. Beat it on the surface by grabbing the dough in halves and creating a crease and by carrying it forward and spreading it, it closes on itself. In such a way, the glutinic mesh will start forming and some air will be incorporated inside. This should be done for at least 10 minutes to avoid the dough from stringing.

6. Leave the dough on the surface covered with a plastic wrap and compact the loaf. After waiting for 10-15 minutes, you will notice that the dough has become silky, more compact and smoother. This is also known as an episode. Put a little flour after removing the central notch and create a loaf.

7. Get 4 portions of about 170 g and without lightening too much, pirate every portion but seal the vortex created at the bottom as well. You will get 4 spherical balls. You can now transfer them to a food box and space them at least by 2 cm.

8. Use a lid to cover and leave them in a cool place to rise for 6-8 hours. Keep checking the leavening from time to time.

9. At this point, work on the filling ingredients. Cut the mozzarella roughly and also cut the fiordilatte in slices then in small pieces. Transfer the ricotta to a bowl; add some water and then work on it until you get creamy and smooth consistent dough. Put the oil to heat once the dough has risen and it will reach at 200 degrees temperature.

10. Use a well-floured stick and take the dough ball by detaching it from the bottom. Use dry hands to spread it after putting in on the surface. You will need to get a disk that is smaller than the usual pizza. In the center, put ¼ of the ricotta leaving 3 cm from the edge clean.

11. Add some mortadella of black pepper that has been grated at the moment, fiordilatte and basil leaves.

12. Then close the crescent pizza using your fingers by squeezing to seal the edges well. Use your fists again to squeeze the edge again and ensure there are no holes. Lift and transfer it to a pan with boiling oil and it will stretch naturally then dip it in hot oil.

13. You can use two skimmers. Keep the pizza immersed using one and move the oil over it using the other. Turn it upside down and keep cooing until its golden brown after waiting for few minutes.

14. Put it on a tray with fried paper after draining it and continue with preparing and cooking others. Serve and enjoy your hot fried pizzas.

Storage:

It is advisable to eat the fried pizza immediately.

Advice:

When you form the balls, tighten them a lot if you want a leavening longer than a couple of hours

Put the dough balls on a tray and use a plastic wrap to cover them if you don't have a food box. It's crucial that they do not take air.

You can make the montanare with the same mixture.

Choose the flour with is between 220 and 260.

You can replace mortadella with salami if you don't like it.

Pear and Brie Pizza

Cook time: 25'
Preparation: 45'
Serves: 4
Cost: Low
Difficulty: Very Easy

Ingredients

- 600 g Water
- 60 g Extra virgin olive oil
- 1 kg Flour 0
- 20 g Salt
- 7 g Dry brewer's yeast

For the dressing
- 30 g PDO Parmesan Cheese
- 200 g Brie
- 400 g Williams pears
- 250 g mozzarella

Directions

1. Begin by pouring the flour into a bowl. Add 100 ml of water yeast and then use a hook mounted at medium-low speed to operate the planetary mixer.

2. Continue by adding water little at a time and make sure you wait till the previous dose is well absorbed by the flour. When you have added at least ¾ of water, keep kneading after adding salt. Always keep adding the rest of the water flush and allow it to work until you get a homogeneous and smooth mixture.

3. Gradually add the oil at this point and remove the dough from the planetary mixer once the oil has absorbed completely and use your hands to shape it until you form a ball. Put it in a lightly greased bowl.

4. Use a clean cloth or a cling film to cover and allow it to rise in the oven while lights are on. Hold on until the dough has doubled in its size but better if tripled and continue with the pizza preparation.

5. Transfer the dough to the pastry board once it rises and divide it in 4 equal

parts. Do this for each of the balls. Let it stand for 30 minutes after covering it with a clean tea towel.

6. Continue by adding water little by little as you wait. On the pizza, pour a drizzle of oil and proceed to seasoning it. Cut the brie into slices a bit more than 5 mm in thickness and then on each side, make small squares of about 2.5 cm. Arrange the coarsely chopped mozzarella on the pizza at this point and then add the brie.

7. Lastly, sprinkle with parmesan and then bake at 200 degrees for 10 minutes. Meanwhile, you can cut and peel the pears. Remove the core after cutting them into slices of equal thickness.

8. Take the pizza out of the oven after 10 minutes and put the pears on the pizza in a radial pattern and bake them again at 200 degrees for another 10-15 minutes.

9. Serve the pear and brie pizza immediately you remove it from the oven.

Storage

You can freeze the pizza after the first cooking. Just add the pears and bring the pizza to the end of cooking once it has been thawed.

Advice

You can add a handful of chopped walnuts if you want to make your pear and brie pizza more delicious. The brie can also be replaced with gorgonzola or taleggio

Pizza with Mortadella and Buffalo Mozzarella

Cook time: 12'

Preparation: 30'

Serves: 2

Cost: Low

Difficulty: Medium

Note: Leavening 16 h

Ingredients

- 500 g 0 Flour
- 300 g Water
- 1 g Fresh brewer's yeast
- 12 g Salt
- 1 tbsp. Extra virgin olive oil

To stuff:
- 100 g Mortadella
- 200 g Buffalo mozzarella
- Basil to taste
- Extra virgin olive oil to taste

Directions

1. To make this pizza with mortadella and buffalo mozzarella, begin by taking care of the dough. In a mixer with a hook, pour in the flour, add yeast and slowly pour the water as you begin working on the dough.

2. Knead the dough and when it begins to string, add salt and water and then keep adding gradually. Add the oil once all the oil has been absorbed completely. Continue kneading the dough until it absorbs that too and starts stringing around the hook.

3. When the dough is soft and smooth. Turn it over on a floured work surface and by rotating the dough between your hands, form a ball and then grease the bowl with oil and lay the dough there.

4. Sprinkle the surface lightly using flour and use a cling film to cover the dough and allow it to rise for 10-12 hours at room temperature because the rising times vary according to the season.

5. Turn the dough on a floured work surface when the leavening is over and divide them in two parts to form a ball and lay them on a kitchen towel. Let it rise until it double in the volume or for about 2 hours.

6. Get a round baking pan with diameter of 32 cm and flour it. Using your hands to spread, put one of the balls in the center until the pan is covered completely and mind to leave the tallest cornice.

7. Get the sheet you previously used to cover the pan. Proceed with the same process for the second pizza. Heat the oven that is possibly ventilated at 250 degrees and on the second track at the bottom, position the grill. Cut the mozzarella buffalo into slices and keep them aside.

8. Season one of the pizzas with the oil necessary to grease the surface once the oven has reached the required temperature and cook for 7-8 minutes.

9. Remove the pizza from the oven and fill it with half of the buffalo that was prepared. Again, bake it for 3-4 minutes, remove it from the oven and fill it with basil to taste and half of the mortadella and continue in the same way for the second pizza.

10. Immediately serve your pizza with mortadella and buffalo.

Storage:

You can cook the pizza bases for 7 minutes if you prefer to keep the pizzas in the freezer. Remove them from the oven and when they are cold, freeze them with bags that are appropriate and just bake them still frozen and continue cooking pers the recipe when you need them, but you may need to increase a few minutes.

Advice:

You may as well serve the pizza with mixed vegetables or chopped pistachios.

Mascarpone Pizza, Speck and Walnuts

Cook time: 30'
Preparation: 15'
Serves: 4
Cost: Low
Difficulty: Easy
Rising Time: 2 h

Ingredients

- 60 g Extra virgin olive oil
- 600 g Water
- 1 kg 0 Flour
- 20 g Salt
- 7 g Dry brewer's yeast

For the stuffing
- 10 g Extra virgin olive oil
- 700 g Tomato sauce
- 150 g Creamy mascarpone
- 10 g Oregano
- 150 g Sliced speck
- 600 g Buffalo mozzarella or fiordilatte
- 40 g Walnut kernels
- Salt to taste

Directions

1. To make the marinara pizza, begin by pouring the flour into a mixer bowl. Add 100 ml of water and yeast and then use a hook mounted at medium-low speed to operate the planetary mixer.

2. Continue by adding water little at a time and make sure you wait till the previous dose is well absorbed by the flour. When you have added at least ¾ of water, keep kneading after adding salt. Always keep adding the rest of the water flush and allow it to work until you get a homogeneous and smooth mixture.

3. Gradually add the oil at this point and remove the dough from the planetary mixer once the oil has absorbed completely and use your hands to shape it

until you form a ball. Put it in a lightly greased bowl.

4. Use a clean cloth or a cling film to cover and allow it to rise in the oven while lights are on. Hold on until the dough has doubled in its size but better if tripled and continue with the pizza preparation.

5. Transfer the dough to a pastry board once it rises and divide it in 4 equal parts. Do this for each of the balls. Use a clean towel to cover and then let it stand for 30 minutes.

6. Grease 4 30 cm diameter pizza pans lightly using a drizzle of oil. In the center of the pan, that's where you should put the ball of the dough and begin squeezing from the center outwards if necessary, slightly pulling the sides.

7. Set aside the pizza you are spreading and roll out another one and let the previous one rest if the dough is too elastic and is returning to the shape it had previously. Try spreading the dough over the entire tray surface.

8. In a large bowl separately, pour the tomato sauce and season with oil, oregano and salt. On the pizza base, pour a generous tomato sauce ladle and let it cover almost the whole area by spreading it in a circular motion and leave a boarder of about 1.5 cm.

9. Chop the mozzarella coarsely and put it on the pizza. With the help of a teaspoon, add the mascarpone.

10. Allow the stuffed pizza to rest for at least 10 minutes and then bake for 15 minutes at 250 degrees in a static oven. Meanwhile, use a knife to lightly chop the nuts.

11. Add the freshly chopped walnuts and speck slices onto the pizza once it's out of the oven. Serve the mascarpone speck and walnut pizza while still hot.

Storage

You can cook the mascarpone and walnut speck pizza halfway and then freeze it. You must thaw it at room temperature in order to use it and also finish cooking it in the oven before serving it.

Advice

You can prepare the mascarpone pizza with speck and white walnuts or without tomato pulp if you want. In such a case, you have to add more mascarpone and mozzarella or use other cheeses like gorgonzola or taleggio depending on your taste.

Wallet Pizza with Salami

Ingredients

- 3 g Dry brewer's yeast
- 440 g Water at room temperature
- 750 g 0 Flour
- 20 g Salt
- To season
- Oregano to taste
- 200 g Spicy salami
- 750 g Mozzarella
- 10 g Salt
- 600 g Tomato pulp
- 30 g Extra virgin olive oil

Cook time: 30'
Preparation: 30'
Serves: 4
Cost: Low
Difficulty: Easy
Rising time: 2-3 h

Directions

1. In preparing the pizza with salami, begin by making the pizza dough. In a mixer bowl, pour in the flour, and 100 ml of water and with a hook at medium-low speed, operate the mixer.

2. Add water slowly by slowly and make sure you wait to add once the previous flour has been absorbed by the flour very well.

3. Add salt and keep kneading once at least ¾ of water have been added. Keep adding the water flush and let it work until you get a homogeneous and smooth mixture.

4. Take the dough out of the planetary at this point and work on it for few minutes on a flat surface so as to favor better the glutinic mesh and then use your hands to shape until you get a ball and put it in a slightly greased bowl.

5. Use a clean towel or a cling film to cover the dough and put it in the oven

with lights on at 26-30 degrees temperature as the maximum. Hold on until the dough at least doubles in the volume. This usually takes like 1 hour and 30 minutes and for it to triple, it takes like 2 to 3 hours.

6. Transfer the dough on the pastry board and divide it in 4 equal parts one it rises. You can use a tarot. Using your hands, form small balls from each of these.

7. Use a clean cloth to cover once you have finished and again allow it rest for 30 minutes. Meanwhile, pour tomato sauce in a bowl and do the seasoning with oregano. Add salt and olive oil and when 30 minutes elapse, pick your dough and start rolling it out.

8. On a floured surface, use your hands to lightly crush a ball and gently pull the dough until the thickness is at least 15 cm.

9. Pass the pizza in a lightly greased pan at this point and use your hands to spread it to cover the whole surface.

10. Distribute the passata on the pizzas, almost covering the whole area and spreading it in circular motion and only leave a boarder of 1.5 cm.

11. In a static preheated oven, bake each pizza for 10 minutes at 250 degrees in the lowest part of the oven. Meanwhile, slice the salami and cut every slice in half.

12. Take out each pizza and add pieces of salami and diced mozzarella. At the same temperature, bake again for 20 minutes and putting the pan in the central shelf of the oven.

13. Take the pizzas out of the oven as soon as they are ready and while still hot, fold them, folding in half and then in half again like a booklet.

14. Serve your pizza with hot salami.

Storage:

This portfolio pizza with salami can be frozen after being brought halfway through cooking. You should thaw it at room temperature in you want to use it and before serving, finish the cooking in the oven.

Advice:

Make this pizza type by varying the salami or cheese type.

In recipes that require little cooking and where you want to increase the characteristics of fresh tomatoes even when it's not a season, use tomato pulp.

Fried Panzerotti

Cook time: 15'
Preparation: 45'
Serves: 20
Cost: Low
Note: Add 2 h for leavening

Ingredients

- 500 g 00 flour
- 15 g Extra virgin olive oil
- 20 g Coarse salt
- 7 g Dry brewer's yeast
- 570 g Lukewarm water
- 500 g Manitoba flour
- 10 g Sugar

For the stuffing:
- 200 g, Tomato sauce
- Oregano to taste
- 500 g Mozzarella
- Salt to taste

For frying:
- Seed oil to taste

Directions

1. In preparing the fried panzerotti, in a large bowl, mix the Manitoba flour and 00 flour. In a little warm water, dissolve the yeast taken from the total dose and also add the sugar.

2. To the flour, add the dissolved yeast and in the water that has remained, melt the coarse salt and on the flour, pour the liquid flush and use your hands to begin mixing the ingredients. Mount the hook and knead at medium speed if you want to use the planetary mixer.

3. Add the oil as well and vigorously mix. Transfer the dough to a pastry board and keep kneading and working on it until you get soft and smooth dough.

4. You can now divide the dough in 20 parts of 80 g each and work on each and every part to form a ball and after that, put them on a tray or a pastry board

where they are well spaced from each other.

5. In an oven that is turned off and the lights are on, cover the dough with a blanket and cloth and let the balls rise until they double in the volume.

6. Meanwhile, prepare the panzerotti filling. In a bowl, mix the tomato puree and mozzarella together after cutting the mozzarella in small cubes. Salt and then season with oregano.

7. In a large pot, heat the seed oil and start preparing the panzerotti once the balls have risen. Use a rolling pin to roll out every ball and give it a round shape with a diameter of approximately 20 cm. At the center, put a generous spoonful of filling.

8. Seal the edges well and close the panzerotti that is forming a crescent by first applying pressure using your fingers and then folding the dough inwardly and lastly using the fork prongs, press in order to avoid the filling to come out during the cooking process.

9. Dip the panzerotti immediately in boiling oil and turn them both sides until they become golden brown.

10. Drain them on the paper towels and serve the fried panzerotti while they are still hot.

Storage:

It is possible to freeze the already stuffed raw panzerotti and fry them while they are still frozen.

We recommend eating them immediately or during the day if you want to taste them while they are still fragrant.

You can keep them for a day and heat them in the oven.

Advice:

You can also try flavoring with salami, anchovies or olives and basil.

If you do not like frying, you may cook them for 20 minutes in a static oven heat at 200 degrees and ventilated at 180 degrees until they become brown on both sides.

Chapter 6: Types of Cooking

There are various oven types when it comes to pizza cooking. The oldest of them all is the traditional wood-burning oven, which was very common before the coming of the gas and electric oven. The wood-burning oven was there when pizza was birthed.

Wood-burning oven

Experience was needed in using the wood-burning oven because managing the wood was not an easy thing. This type of oven did not have a thermometer to check the temperature. People would rely on the refractory walls and their color. At the start, the color of the oven (cold oven) would be dark, it would then turn to almost red and it would finally turn white when the ideal temperature was reached. The ideal temperature for cooking a classic pizza using a wood oven is 450° - 485° and the time for cooking is about 1 minute and 30 seconds for Neapolitan pizza. The mouth's relationship with the chamber's overall volume is of great importance. This is where the pizza-cooking skill of the baker came in because for some, such as the filling, had to be cooked in the "oven mouth" so as to melt the mozzarella inside, combining with the rest of the ingredients and ensure that the pasta is not burnt. The consumption of the wood varies between 4-5 kg for every hour. Another problem with this type of oven is that it needs lots of space to be installed.

Electric oven

Electric ovens vary depending on model. It is recommended to use a static electric oven for a pizzeria where the air naturally circulates and the air is not forced out. Convention through the lower cooking surface is the main system of cooking. Radiation is also part of the cooking whereby the upper resistances emit heat. There is also further cooking by heating the oven air. It is the type of oven used in rotisserie pizzerias. Due to its simplicity of use, even a person without much experience can operate this oven.

Gas ovens

These ovens are the same as the wood ovens and static ones are used for pizzerias. The pros off the gas ovens are that you can quickly regulate the temperature, shorter period for heating, and more hygienic and cheaper consumptions than previous ones. With the burner invention, the gas ovens are increasingly used in pizzerias because the equipment put under the cooking chamber heats upwards from the bottom. The burner makes the floor to heat up more than the ceiling of the chamber.

Analyzing the three ovens, I can say that there are chefs who like the wood oven because they have the required skills to manage the oven.

With tricks of a chef, the gas oven can make a pizza almost the same as the one made using a wood oven. There are course differences, which are not easily noticeable.

The electric does not convince many people because the dough turns out too dry, and this makes it lose its softness and hydration. However, this is just a view of some people and there are others that like it very much.

How to Cook Pizza in the Home Oven?

The preparation of the dough is very important in making the pizza at home.

For those whose oven is not ventilated, you are advised to cook it for five minutes at the bottom and then move it to the middle off the oven.

If you have a ventilated oven, cook at the center. The reason for this is the heat becomes violent with the fan oven and therefore the cooking time is reduced. For such a case, put the pizza in half.

The pan that you choose to use also plays an important role.

In order to homogeneously cook the pizza above and below, you need to get a slab of refractory stoneto. It gives a crunchy pizza and with a fragrance like in a pizzeria.

On the bottom of the oven, you can use the refractory stone as it will help in keeping the temperature high even when the oven is opened.

Cook the pizza for the initial 6-7 minutes on the lower part if you are experimenting

Cooking Temperature

To get a good pizza, the best temperature range is 380-450 °C when using a wooden oven. For the gas oven, it is recommended to use temperatures not exceeding 250 °. It works the same as the wooden oven.

Cooking Time for Homemade Pizza

It takes about 3-5 minutes to cook a pizza in a professional gas oven or an electric oven. It takes about 15-20 minutes using a classic oven. To know when the pizza is ready, check the edges and see if they have started caramelizing, becoming golden.

It takes 45 minutes to get the right temperature when using a wood oven, but it will take even more than an hour for the oven to be ready if the wood oven is rarely used.

A pizza can be cooked in just less than a minute in a plate using a wood oven at the right temperature. You need to continuously turn it as it quickly darkens on the side off the flame.

Tips for the perfect pizza:

1. Ensure that the right flour is used. Strong flour is important for a long

leavening.

2. Do not contact salt with the yeast. The salt sterilizes the yeast's action, as it is a disinfectant.

3. Water temperature. The water should not be very hot. The yeast will be sterilized by heat. You can also use cold water.

4. Container. Use the right special container and spread the pizza in it. It is not recommended to use the oven tray as its bottom is thick which makes it hard to cook the lower part.

5. Do not use a rolling pin. Use your hands to spread the pizza as a rolling pin breaks the bubbles that leaven to making the dough crumbly and light.

6. Use a good oven to prepare the pizza.

Mistakes to Avoid when Cooking Homemade Pizza

In making a homemade pizza, there are several mistakes that you need to avoid in order to make a perfect one. Here are those mistakes and how to avoid them.

Yeast: Are you using the right yeast?

The yeast is undoubtedly important for preparing and cooking of a great pizza. The yeast used by many expert pizza chefs is the mother yeast, which is very famous. You can alternatively use granulated yeast.

Usually there is a greater rising time when the amount of yeast is lower. Some people have also developed the custom of letting the dough rise in a fridge.

Choosing the Flour: is one worth the other?

Absolutely not. Quality flour brings forth quality pizza. Flour 0 is highly recommended buy pizza chefs. It is recommended to use a mixture with Manitoba flour if the dough is very soft. It is recommended that you by the flour from the mill in order to get dough of high quality.

Should the salt be added? If yes, when?

Yes, the salt can be added, but at the end. This is because the salt sterilizes the yeast's action, as it is a disinfectant.

Do I need to add sugar?

Yes, it is a very important ingredient, which can stimulate leavening and should be added to the yeast. You can alternatively use malt or honey.

Rolling Pin; should I use it?

It is highly recommended to use a rolling pin for a homemade pizza, more so if you cannot use your hand to roll the dough out. Lots of delicacy is needed in this process, especially this part.

What is the reason behind the so much melting of mozzarella in homemade pizza?

There is a lot of whey in a classic mozzarella and this is why there is a lake effect avoided often when cooking homemade pizza. The remedy for this is cutting the mozzarella in slices and putting it for 2-3 hour in a colander.

Is it right to fill the pizza with other ingredients before you bake it?

No, it is wrong. If you fill the ingredients before baking, they will burn even before baking. It is ideal baking the pizza with tomato only, and when about to end cooking, add mozzarella and then the ingredients. Ham should come in at the end.

What is the ideal temperature?

Given that the cooking temperature for pizzas is pizzerias is about 300°, this kind of heat cannot be used in a domestic oven. You can use the maximum temperature of the oven, putting the pizza at the lowest part possible.

Tips to Make the Perfect Pizza

These tips will help you craft the perfect pizza. They will keep your cooking running smoothly and allow you to focus on your guests.

1. Perfect pizza comes from hand shaping. Avoid relying on a rolling pin to create a thin crust. To get a feel for properly proofed dough, stretch

it by hand.

2. If the dough seems unwilling to maintain its shape on your peel and is noticeably contracting, wait about five minutes for the gluten to relax and then gently stretch it a bit more. I'm generally not too concerned with shape; round or oval tastes the same but thickness counts. Thin to win is my mantra.

3. Less is more when it comes to saucing and topping pizzas. Weighty, wet ingredients cause the dough to steam rather than spring to life. A limp, undercooked pie just will not do.

4. Finish like a pro. Keep a small ramekin of chopped garlic covered in olive oil on your prep station. Finish the cooked pizza by brushing the crust with a thin coat of garlic oil for added flavor and a glossy crust.

5. The best pizzas are made in a hot, bright oven, meaning a fully engaged fire with flames that roll over the dome and a fully heated floor. Add a slender split log directly to the fire if there is no active flame, and let it ignite before baking a pie.

6. After 10 to 15 pizzas, most ovens will experience a drop in floor temperature. Reheat the floor by raking the embers back over the cooking surface and allow it to stand for 10 minutes. Push the fire aside, add a thin log to the embers, and allow it to ignite; then resweeps the floor and resume turning out crispy pies.

7. Some ingredients need to be cooked before topping a raw pizza; they won't properly finish in the short amount of time the dough spends in the oven. Precook thinly sliced vegetables such as potatoes and eggplant. Other ingredients, such as greens and mushrooms, can contain a lot of water, and should also be precooked so they don't weigh down your pizza.

Conclusion

You now know what the basic parts of each homemade Italian pizza, how to make them and how to assemble your very own gustatory masterpiece. Now, you can have your pizza and eat it too at a much lower price than ordering out…all in the comfort of your own home.

But as knowledge is only half the battle, the things you learned in this book is just, well, half the pizza. To make it whole, you'll need to actually try them out. Start by making the dough, one of the sauce recipes and 3 toppings. And if your first experiment doesn't turn out as you expected, note what you think did not work and try again differently. Try and try until you pie.

I sincerely hope that the book has succeeded in its mission to stop depending on commercial pizzas and prepare them at home with easy to follow instructions.

Made in the USA
Monee, IL
28 November 2020